LIVING DIVINE LOVE

Transformation, the Goal of Christian Life

LIVING DIVINE LOVE

Transformation, the Goal of Christian Life

by

Dominic M. Hoffman, O.P.

ALBA · HOUSE   NEW · YORK

SOCIETY OF ST. PAUL, 2187 VICTORY BLVD., STATEN ISLAND, NEW YORK 10314

248.4
HOL

Library of Congress Cataloging in Publication Data

Hoffman, Dominic M., 1913-
  Living divine love.

  1. Spiritual life—Catholic authors. I. Title.
BX2350.2.H583   1982   248.4'82   82-11552
ISBN 0-8189-0443-7

Nihil Obstat:
James T. O'Connor, S.T.D.
Censor Librorum

Imprimatur:
†Joseph T. O'Keefe, D.D.
Vicar General, Archdiocese of New York
September 3, 1982

Designed, printed and bound in the United States of
America by the Fathers and Brothers of the
Society of St. Paul, 2187 Victory Boulevard,
Staten Island, New York 10314, as part of their
communications apostolate.

---

1 2 3 4 5 6 7 8 9 (Current Printing: first digit).

To
St. Thérèse of Lisieux,
A Light to the Church—
In Return for Much.

CONTENTS

INTRODUCTION

The simple and consoling thing about the last stages of the spiritual life is, that they are not essentially different from the first. In the beginning we learned that we must love God above all things with a great and personal love. We must try to see him as a person to whom we mean much and who is intensely interested in us. We also learned that we must love our neighbor or we fail in the love of this same God. All this is made easier by the fact of the God-man, both as we see him in the gospels and as we actually meet him in the Blessed Sacrament.

In the last stages of the spiritual life these essentials are not different. We must still love God above all things with a personal love, and we understand more than ever how unbelievably he is involved in us. We find our way to him through Christ, and with the Blessed Sacrament our life-giving spiritual food, the Real Presence is our great joy and refuge, where love of neighbor increases with love of God.

The difference is not one of kind but of degree, although the degree of intensity of love and closeness to God is so much greater. People may be pardoned for thinking that later supernatural love is really different from earlier supernatural love and that the indwelling of God by grace can have different essential species. Yet the same things we had in hand as we began the spiritual journey will still be our life when we finish, but always in greater perfection and in greater union. The whole life of grace is one life, and this should help to make it less mysterious.

The matters of the later spiritual life are admittedly hard to write about, not always because they are so complex, but rather because they are so simple. For, who can adequately describe what is meant by union or oneness, or by love and great love? Such things are experiences we live, rather than things we can tell about, or at times even ought to tell about. Here the secrets of the King can be very great and very precious. In matters of the intimate spiritual life, we should not dare to speak of them unless God sometimes willed it otherwise. Within certain limits they are not entirely inaccessible to human words and language.

This book is not principally a detailed description of the phenomena accompanying the particular state of soul. Rather it is our primary intention to establish a few central ideas and to give some practical advice. There are objective principles which may have escaped even some of those who have traveled a great distance up the mountain. There are also counsels, and even warnings, because the ascent now becomes more dangerous in the sense that a slip now can have greater consequences. At this time in the spiritual life a mistaken path may be all but irreparable for reaching the summit so long desired.

This book must be judged for what it is, principally an explanation of the spiritual life as seen from the point of view of its perfection. By itself, it is not a complete treatment of the spiritual or Christian life. With the other books which we have written on the spiritual life it forms one whole. The omissions which were necessary here to bring out the theme of this book must be sought in the earlier books. This one is to be interpreted in the light of the others. Thus, the present book concentrates primarily on the relationship of God and the individual soul, but this does not mean that now at this stage the Christian man or woman can neglect the love and duties toward others. Yet in the contemporary situation of the Church it is an affirmation that our perfection as followers of Christ, lies more in the union with God than with our neighbor, although there must always be a harmony between the two.

Although in these pages we intend to discuss only the final part of the spiritual life, which ends with the transforming union or the spiritual marriage, this book is by no means restricted to the chosen few. The Second Vatican Council has settled the doubts anyone might have had about the call to holiness. Emphatically all are called. "The Lord Jesus, the divine Teacher and Model of perfection, preached holiness of life to each and every one of his disciples, regardless of their situation: 'You are therefore to be perfect, even as your heavenly Father is perfect' (Mt 5:48). He himself stands as the Author and Finisher of this holiness of life. He sent the Holy Spirit upon all people that He might inspire them from within to love God with their whole heart and their whole soul, with all their mind and all their strength, and that they might love one another as Christ loved them. . . . Thus it is evident to everyone that all the faithful of Christ of whatever rank or status, are called to the fullness of the Christian life and to the perfection of charity. By this holiness a more human way of life is promoted even in this earthly society" (*Constitution on the Church*, no. 40).

This book has an implicit interest for everyone concerned with the spiritual life. Without forgetting that there are many steps on the way, it does give even to a beginner, a firm confidence in the value of the steps he is now taking. He is, in a sense, not walking blindly as if he did not see the end, or see it put in reasonable and understandable terms.

Since the same principles in general operate throughout the spiritual life, there is a decided encouragement in seeing that they are able to bring him to the end of it. Also, in seeing what is useful for the rest of the journey, he may be able to discard sooner, with more freedom of spirit, any unnecessary burden and the impediments which he mistakenly may be carrying.

In the intermingling of principles and practice, we will be guided by those in the Church who have received her special approval in matters of the later spiritual life. The firm and profound principles of St. Thomas Aquinas must have first place, because of the general approval given him above all the other doctors of the Church, and also because these principles were able to make him a saint and a man of much mystical experience, even though not a mystical writer in the accepted sense.

In addition we must depend heavily on the writings of the two saints usually associated with these last stages, St. John of the Cross and St. Teresa of Avila. There are also two other well-known saints who have written of themselves. One will not cause great surprise, St. Thérèse of Lisieux. She has given us an intimate account of her inner life in many respects quite different from the other two. By a canceling out of dissimilarities, we will be able more easily to see what is the essence of the states with which we are concerned.

Although he should have been mentioned first, the second of the additional authorities is so neglected that it will cause some surprise to those who read mystical literature. This most excellent source of principles and practice in the ultimate stages of the spiritual life is St. Paul, a man confirmed in grace. In many of the lines of his letters he gives us a glimpse into his inner soul. We see from them what it is to be a saint and how a saint can act and feel. We find a living human being and not a painted-over image of what a saint ought to be. These two saints, St. Paul and St. Thérèse, may make us alter some of our impressions, but the change of mind will free us, in many cases, from futile striving after the impossible.

Any misdirection may lead toward an ideal which is objectively unreal, or (in God's plan for the individual) impossible. This plan of God, or the personal vocation, has been a recurring theme in all we have previously written and it reaches its summit here. The spiritual life is like a seed planted in each of us at baptism and is intended to be brought to perfection—but not to all the varieties of perfection, nor to perfection in general, nor to anyone else's perfection. In God's plan, and *within the boundaries he has laid out for all Christian perfection and for our state in life*, each one of us is destined to glorify him, not only by an exterior life lived according to God's individual pattern for each, but even more in an interior life of God's design. This uniqueness of plan will be matched by graces which will bring us to that emphasis, which is our personal way of coming to him.

It also seems that by the idea of personal vocation, much of the controversy can be settled concerning various means and characteristics of spiritual perfection such as, for instance, the necessity of great amounts of contemplative prayer according to a schedule that leads in a rigorously categorized crescendo to ever higher and higher forms of it. Various capacities are given to each of us by God, and our perfection is to find them and to fulfill those which in his wisdom he chooses to have us fulfill, even as he chose to fulfill only some of the human potentialities of Christ. His way for us, for instance, no matter how high he may draw us in mystical prayer, then becomes the ordinary way for us. This is a valid personalism, firmly integrated with the entire and eternal plan of God.

We have tried to keep the language clear and nontechnical whenever possible. Similarly the reader will not find this a greatly poetic book like that of St. John of the Cross, nor one fired by flights of the imagination. It is simple, expository writing.

Neither is the book an account of subjective experience. If one is a Teresa of Avila, or someone like this remarkable woman, a personal account has a valid place. But a realistic assessment of oneself, as well as of some of what is currently being written, compels the judgment that the injection of the personal would be only of passing interest, if any. Rather the book is the fruit of much objective study, experience and thought, and for this reason it applies to many more people—one of the best of all reasons for writing such a book, as well as for reading it.

PART I

THE NATURE OF THE TRANSFORMING UNION

Chapter 1

CONCERNING THE
SPIRITUAL MARRIAGE

Since we cannot speak with the tongues of angels, who see everything clearly and accurately, we must be content to speak with the tongues of men. Yet the tongues of men, ever since Babel, have created language of communication, and also language which fails to communicate or which communicates poorly. This last situation is, in some sense, unavoidable in the later spiritual life. Men and women describe their experiences with God, and as a result a certain terminology grows up, hallowed both by reason of its sainted users and by the repetition of time. It is a language filled with symbolism, because these experiences are difficult to put into any other words, and also because as men, we must find a certain psychological fulfillment in that union of spirit and earth which is the symbol.

Necessary and valuable though these expressions are, we find that they are vague, instead of precise and that they are metaphors rather than something concrete, which we can relate to the reality which we ourselves may experience. Matters are left in this state both because of the reverence for those who have gone before, and because there is an understandable lack of will to change what one has not himself experienced. For instance, what nonscientific layman among us would venture to correct the sometimes obscure terminology of the sciences?

Yet it seems that such an attempt must be made if we are not to remain vague, if we are to succeed in these last steps of the spiritual life. For, the end always has this importance, that it gives the reason, purpose, or motive for all the rest. If, therefore, the final stages of the spiritual life are left as metaphors, we may find it a language of confusion, almost a language that deceives. One such expression is the symbol often used to describe the final state of the spiritual man, the spiritual marriage.

The term "spiritual marriage" is a metaphor but it has a foundation in fact. Just as in human marriage the two become so close that the Scripture describes them as one flesh, so can we become one with God in the spirit—except, of course, that the reality of intensely experiencing God's love transcends any symbol. Understood in this way, it is a valid and immensely useful concept for everyone. In its essence it deals with realities with which we all are familiar: first, with the soul and God, and then also, with close union and still individual separateness, something again with which we are all familiar in the ideal of marriage. If all else connected with this symbol could be seen as extraneous to this essence, there would be little reason to question it.

Yet a term is rarely understood solely in its essential meaning. Most often it must be accepted along with other associations which come from usage in the past sometimes more than in the present. There are two such sources of usage which extend the meaning of the term "spiritual marriage" to more than the simple close union of the soul with God. Both of these laudable sources extend the term to union with Christ, the God-man. They are: first, certain interpretations of *The Canticle of Canticles* (or *The Song of Songs*) in the Old Testament, and second, the experience of some of the female saints.

As to the first, the interpretation of *The Canticle of Canticles*: the expression "spiritual marriage" gained its great acceptance from an extension of the allegorical interpretation of this inspired poem. Originally the allegory seems to have been limited to God as the bridegroom and the Chosen People as the bride. In Christian times this relationship was logically transformed into the love of Christ and his Church, following consistent references by Christ to himself as bridegroom. The beautiful language of the poem also opens itself to a further extension, to the love of God, or of Christ and the individual soul. The development of this personal allegory of the soul and Christ, reached its highest point in the sermons of St. Bernard. Even centuries later, they are able to melt the soul.

It is especially in this concept of Christ as bridegroom and the soul as bride that the term "spiritual marriage" can become a difficulty to the very large male segment of those in the spiritual life. The whole of humanity is asked to desire union with Christ in a terminology which directly affects only half of it. For a woman, to become the spiritual spouse of Christ through spiritual marriage is a direct, simple, and normally appealing objective. But a man does not instinctively think of Christ in such a way, even though in the unitive stage of the spiritual life there is sometimes great delight in the growing perception of the Sacred Humanity. Instead the response is more apt to be that of man to God and man to man, which is to say of friend to friend or of heart to heart, for instance, like the love of St. Paul for Christ. And although this kind of friendship with Christ can have unbelievable depths, it does not denote the all-absorbing emotional depth and intensity that a woman ideally feels in the marriage situation. Thus, what a man feels (or is told to expect) at the end of the spiritual life, is not always accurately described as the spiritual marriage.

The second source of the acceptance of this term is the experience of some of the female saints. In them the spiritual marriage has not just been a metaphor derived indirectly from the Scripture. It has been a real experience under the symbol of an actual marriage with Christ, for instance, an actual ceremony with the giving of a ring. If we have read about such descriptions, there is no doubt that our reaction toward the summit of the spiritual life is conditioned by such accounts, whether in unconscious anticipation or perhaps, on the contrary, in rejection.

It will help, in either case, to be told that the experiences of these saints were personal to them as individuals, that this was God's way of symbolizing the spiritual union with these few, whereas, no such experience came to other saints whom, we may surely believe, loved God at least equally well. The inescapable suspicion is that, because of the association with such descriptions and because of the allegories of the soul and Christ based on *The*

Canticle of Canticles, the spiritual male may become estranged or confused, at least unconsciously, in his desire for the reality, the closest possible relationship with God and with Christ in this life.

Thus the term "spiritual marriage," to be used with any degree of universality, must be stripped of all but its essential, spiritual meaning, that of the final and highest union of the soul with God in this life. But even here, where it is not the figure of marriage to Christ, but rather of the soul to God, can we say that it is always a totally acceptable approach for the spiritual male to take to God? The idea of the bride is always feminine and a man cannot habitually adopt the attitudes of a woman without risking the loss of his basically masculine personality. He must not, even from the very beginning, expect that the spiritual life will make him any less a man, for grace builds upon nature and does not destroy it. But unfortunately, this is what the symbol of the bride may tend to do. Thus, the man ought not to expect that at the summit of the spiritual life, he will psychologically feel love from God or for God in the same way that a woman does.

It is true, so far as the figure of marriage goes, that the symbol of the soul as bride makes use of the most intense love experience that human nature knows. For, the totality of absorption of one being into another, which is characteristic of the woman in ideal married love, does very vividly express in human, and easily understood terms, the wholeness of giving to God to which all should aspire.

It is the very force of this image, however, which may be the source of its limitations. In these latter days our sexuality is more clearly defined and more deeply appreciated as the gift of God that it is (and an inalienable gift besides) even though according to our vocation we may give back to God our use of it. Also, in the case of many men it is more acutely under psychological stress than it was in former times. Therefore, it is at least questionable whether it would be wise for a man continually to conceive of his soul and its love attitudes as feminine. We do not go to God only as "souls," although this is the part of us that directly touches the supernatural life of grace. We go as the whole person.

The man's approach to the object of his natural love, that is, to the woman, is in the main different from her approach to him. He is by nature, by the design of God, more aggressive in his basic love pattern. He tends to go out toward the woman, to possess her. On her part, she tends more toward receiving love, or better, toward joyfully surrendering to it. She possesses by being possessed.

These are only general, though fundamental, observations. Human love is not rigidly confined to one pattern. Quite naturally and beautifully there are spontaneous variations upon the roles of the man and the woman in married love, and this is done without psychological harm, but rather with consequent increase of love. This is to be expected since both sexes are compositely male and female. In the context of the life of prayer, it is quite possible that, with a man, his soul may be caught up in prayer, in a rapture for instance, to which he can only surrender.

This partial sharing of the opposite sexual nature, however, does not argue for a continual exchange of the natural roles in loving. Since grace and our basic nature act in harmony, the man can be close to God only to the extent that he is authentically what he is, a male. Any deep frustration of a natural psychological drive could become an obstruction to the increasing union with God. The psyche (the whole spiritual-material, knowing, willing, and feeling part of man) would adhere to God imperfectly like a piece of sticking tape when portions of it do not stick because no moisture is applied to them.

Once all this is clearly understood, it can easily be seen that it is not necessary for the man in his spiritual reading or praying to identify himself with the female symbol of the bride. It would ordinarily seem enough that he appreciate the force of the symbol and be moved toward God and the God-man Christ because of the intense oneness that it implies, or that he love God according to his own nature, but with an intensity which could be described in a spiritual sense only as if it were love for a spouse.

Yet, despite all that we have said, the truth is that for some men, the image of the spiritual marriage has been helpful, and we have saints to prove it. St. Bernard and St. John of the Cross are good examples. And so, generally, within the limits of the purely spiritual union of the soul with God, and abstracting from vivid personal imagery involving the feminine, and abstracting also from a predominantly feminine psychological approach to God, we may say that even for men the symbol of the spiritual marriage can have a limited, but great usefulness.

Despite the beauty and usefulness of this figure, however, spiritual marriage between God and the individual soul is not a symbol directly used in the Scriptures. The closest we come to it in the Old Testament is the language of the prophets in which God describes his love for the Chosen People. This is probably true also in *The Canticle of Canticles*, but since this love poem has been interpreted in a personal sense for so long in the Church, we can surely accept personal union as a meaning which God also intended in it. In the New Testament the same symbol of marriage is also used for the union of God and the Church, both in St. Paul (2 Cor 11:2) and in the Apocalypse or Revelation (21:2). It is in this sense that Christ referred to himself as the bridegroom (Mt 9:15) with the Church as bride, and this is also the primary meaning of the parable of the Ten Virgins (Mt 25:1). Thus we may say without fear of serious contradiction that the symbol of spiritual marriage even though it ought to be retained in every acceptable sense, was not given by God directly. In fact he gave us another.

Chapter 2

CHILDREN OF THE KINGDOM

The various concepts and symbols of spiritual perfection can sometimes lead us a long way from the perfection we seek. They also can repel outsiders from any desire or hope for perfection. In our day, we do not so easily follow the errors of those who would surround the idea of sanctity with supposedly inseparable characteristics such as severe penances, miracles, visions, long hours of prayer, and great apostolic or, charitable works. But some unfortunate effects of the idea of spiritual marriage do not so easily leave us. Somehow, even if we need not swoon in ecstasy like St. Catherine of Siena, we still ought to be able to feel in the grand manner of St. Teresa of Avila or St. John of the Cross, as if we were already among the seraphim. Perhaps, this is the reason that our Lord chose to give us as a symbol of our highest perfection, one that enables us more to be ourselves. This image he has given us in answer to the question we are considering, when we speak of spiritual perfection: "Who is the greatest in the kingdom of heaven?", that is, in the kingdom which is the Church on earth, as well as in heaven. The answer, of course is familiar: "The one who makes himself as little as this little child, is the greatest in the kingdom of heaven." (Mt 18:1 ff).

The idea of the child as a symbol of spiritual perfection, is not without natural repugnance for some people. The spiritual man is still a man, and as an adult he may not like to think himself reduced to the helplessness of a child. But, this is only to say that the spiritual man is a fallen man. He must constantly struggle with the same temptation which overcame Adam in the Garden and is one of the most appealing aspects of atheism and secularism, the temptation to complete self-sufficiency and to independence from God. And yet, here it is from the lips of Christ, that to become perfect, we must become like children.

To reassure ourselves, however, we have the personalities of those who have been given the grace to become perfect. We see our Lord himself, a strong, yet gentle, masculine figure. St. Paul is not an immature child either. The women are illustriously represented by two flames of fire, St. Catherine of Siena and St. Teresa of Avila—not to continue with an unending list of others from both sexes. These assure us that we do not become less adult men and women by becoming children before God. Indeed, in becoming this kind of child, we will see many of our immaturities disappear.

Spiritual childhood essentially means a recognition of basic truth, the Allness of God. From the creation of the universe down to our own creation, and in the providence which rules the earth while it permeates each of our lives, there is a necessary dependence upon God as First Cause. He is First Cause in every order of being, both of grace and of nature. It is an untruth to deny this; it is living the truth to accept it. Our Lord told us flatly, "Without me you can do nothing" (Jn 15:5). Dependency is written in every part of our nature, and in every act flowing from that nature, whether we can recognize this or not.

Added to this is the enormous dependency coming from personal defects of our own making. This last, we have all experienced and in childlike honesty we will admit it. Since, therefore, we cannot accomplish spiritual growth without God's help, then quite clearly those who more deeply recognize their essential and personal dependence will be able to become the more perfect.

No one knows better than the person who has attained some degree of spiritual perfection that total dependence is not mere passivity. It is putting ourselves into the rhythm by which the universe is run. God must give help toward every action. And in the spiritual life, as in our activity in the world, the joint work of God's will and our own is always toward building up a perfection that is maturely human "until we come to the perfect man, fully mature with the fullness of Christ himself" (Ep 4:13).

To understand the full value of the child symbol, we must first understand what it means. Quite obviously our Lord is not referring to the qualities of children, which would be undesirable for mature men and women, such as lack of intelligence or, inner discipline. Even more, surely he is not referring to the bad qualities of some children, such as, inconstancy of will, obstinacy, and selfishness. Childhood for him is synonymous with sinlessness.

Nor is Christ overlooking certain differences between the order of nature and the order of grace. By nature we are given childhood in the beginning, almost all at once, whereas grace impels us toward spiritual childhood by degrees of maturity, by spiritual growth. Nature moves us irrevocably toward independence from our parents, but grace draws us toward ever greater dependence upon our heavenly Father.

Spiritual childhood has two essential aspects: the willingness to be taught and the trustful recognition of our need for God's help in everything. As such, the symbol does not describe spiritual perfection, but rather shows the way to spiritual perfection—and psychological perfection as well. It does not, by itself, symbolize the love of God, as the bride does, nor the heroic degree of the virtues, as does the fullness of the humanity of Christ. But it does provide us with the way to acquire all these: by being taught and by trustfully expecting the help and care of God. Because we are like children we will acquire all else. This is what is meant by receiving the kingdom of God as a child. And, "Whoever does not receive the kingdom of God as a little child shall not enter into it" (Mk 10:15). The first requirement for receiving his kingdom is basic faith. The fullness of this kingdom is the perfection of spiritual childhood.

In the two essential aspects of spiritual childhood, we can see the difference between the symbols of the child and those of the bride. As to the first aspect, the willingness to be taught, children are eminently capable of being taught, whereas the bride or the friend is often the teacher. We shall have much need of being taught throughout the spiritual life. We are continuously being taught by God through deeper understanding of his inspired word, the Scriptures. None of us is ever exempted from being taught by the Church. This is true even in the latter stages of the spiritual life. The short-sighted spirit of self-determination, arising from self-love or pride, is still a danger here. God is always teaching us throughout our lives, indeed is teaching us by means of life itself, as it follows its inexorable rhythm from youth to old age. Thus the unconscious assumption of a false equality which we may associate with the bride or the friend, is countered by the essential and unavoidable dependence of the child.

The difference between the child and the bride, is also shown by the second essential aspect of spiritual childhood, which is the willingness and confidence in accepting the help of God. The bride is surely the helpmate, whereas the child is the dependent. Thus, the bride better describes assiduousness in pleasing God and doing for God. But using that symbol alone can make us neglect the deeper necessity, the dependence upon God both for the perfection of oneself and for the works of duty and charity.

From these considerations we not only see the more basic fittingness of the symbol of the child, but we also must conclude that more than one symbol is required to describe Christian perfection. Any one metaphor is always incomplete, and must never be allowed to obscure the whole reality. The various symbols supplement one another; each indicates one aspect of the never exhausted, always unfolding wonder of the relationship of each soul with God.

The perfect person is always a more complex being than any one symbol. The New Testament gives us a few others to show this. Our Lord gives us: "I send you out as sheep (or lambs) in the midst of wolves" (Mt 10:10; Lk 10:4). "Be wise as serpents and innocent as doves" (Mt ib.). And then sheep in another simile: "I am the door for the sheep ... My sheep hear my voice, and I know them and they know me" (Jn 10:7, 27). Also "I am the vine, you are the branches" (Jn 15:5). Also we are the "good seed" and the "wheat": "the good seed is the children of God" (Mt 13:24, 25, 38). But not only symbols of earth: "Is it not written in your law, 'I said you are gods'?" (Ps 81:6). "If he called them gods to whom the word of God came . . ." (Jn 10:35).

St. Paul is a source of still other symbols: "You are the body of Christ, and individually members of it" (1 Cor 12:27). "You are God's field, God's building. . . . You are God's temple" (1 Cor 3:10, 6). The symbol of the soldier is one of his favorites: "Take your share of suffering as a good soldier of Christ" (2 Tm 2:3). And this is reinforced by frequent references to things military: "Take the shield of faith . . . the helmet of salvation, and the sword of the spirit, which is the word of God" (Ep 6:16, 17). Spiritual adulthood resounds in his epistles and he is particularly fond of the word "sons." Similarly he is aware of the undesirable aspects of childhood (which some mistake for maturity): "Let us be children no longer, tossed here and there, carried about by every wind of doctrine that originates in human trickery and skill in proposing error" (Ep 4:14). Yet, he does not forget that we are to be "blameless children of God" (Ph 2:15), as indeed his Master repeated on occasions other than the ones already mentioned. (See Mt 5:9, 45; Lk 6:35).

The evident truth is that we must be all these things all at once, and much more besides. We remain adults while becoming children. In the two symbols we have been discussing, the soul becomes the bride by becoming the child. In being the bride, it is pre-eminently the child. The same can be said of the friend, except that friendship with God is not a symbol.

The profound dependence on God, as imaged by the child, will not leave us weak. On the contrary, while we depend on God, more and more as we grow closer to him, we also grow into a maturity by which we, more and more become ourselves. We become better able to recognize our true gifts and better able to use them as they must be used, only under God's grace and direction, even when this direction is expressed through others.

Spiritual childhood is always opposed to pride and excessive self-confidence. It symbolizes many virtues, but it especially indicates the one essential to both the spiritual and apostolic life, that of true and unostentatious humility. It thus does away with the self-centeredness and unreliability, which we may have carried from our natural childhood, into adult immaturity. Thus also it brings inner peace, perhaps its most prominent characteristic.

Contrary to natural childhood, we become less self-sufficient, despite the increasing awareness of our true gifts. We do not accept our gifts from God, and then go off to use them as if there were no more need of God. Instead, we humbly recognize that we need his help every moment, even with our greatest gifts. We need him in order to avoid the mistakes which would ruin them, to overcome the obstacles which would impede them, and to suppress the pride which would debase them. We become more supernaturally dependent upon God, not only for interior graces for each moment, but also for external graces, that is, for the people, things, and situations which he puts into our lives to indicate and to help his purposes. This dependence and expectancy of help should not prevent our full human development and operation. In the full practice of the spritual life, we always have Christ as our model. To grow into Christ, is ever a challenge to further personal development and to our powers of action. St. Paul would warn us of a false idea of spiritual childhood: "Do not be children in intelligence. In malice, on the contrary, be childlike, but in intelligence be full-grown men" (1 Cor 14:20). And yet, "Be imitators of God as beloved children" (Ep 5:1).

In spiritual childhood we remain ourselves. We never adopt the mannerisms of an imaginary child (or do so rarely, even when talking to God). We do not attain spiritual childhood by becoming a child in our imagination, or by putting it on, as we do our clothes. This would be regressing into immaturity, and would produce a false image of ourselves. True spiritual childhood flows naturally out of the true self within.

When we have the opportunity to compare people to what they were as children, we often see a regression in regard to character, personality, and even in the use of talents. The fruit does not fulfill the promise of the blossom. On the contrary, by avoiding the weak compromises, the pretense, and the cynicism by which this loss is effected, spiritual childhood keeps us our true selves and produces an authentic adult. We keep ourselves constantly open to the forming and maturing action of grace, as it works through and with the multitudinous circumstances of each life. We remain spiritually one thing with the true person as each of us was designed by the creating mind of God.

Thus spiritual childhood gives us an image or symbol of holiness, which enables us to be ourselves in a mature simplicity, instead of vainly trying (or hopelessly despairing) to be someone else. And since no extraordinary experiences are suggested by this simple and attainable ideal, everyone who sincerely desires the spiritual life, can reasonably believe that he is on his way to its summit, and will with great confidence press on toward it.

Chapter 3

UNION TRANSFORMING

To return once more to the term "spiritual marriage," we may encounter a final difficulty from its use, a difficulty arising from the essence of the spiritual life itself. It is not a difficulty of direct opposition, as if two trains were approaching on the same track, but rather as if two trains were going in the same direction on different tracks. From the Scriptures and from the teachings of the Church, we learn that the ultimate basis of the spiritual life is oneness with God through participation, though as creatures, in his nature. This union and this participation are theologically called sanctifying grace. These three, union, participation, and grace, are all capable of endless increase while we are in this life. In closer union and greater participation we are approaching the idea of spiritual marriage, taken in its essential meaning of soul and God.

We now understand clearly that this union and participation come about principally by love, by the infused virtue of charity if you will. This love, too, knows no limits; it is capable of indefinite increase in this life. Love, under the influence of actual grace, is the greatest unitive force between ourselves and God. Love is principally what draws him down to us and draws us up to him; and we are told that by increasing in love, we will become saints, all something very simple and understandable. It is in this context that the first two stages of the spiritual life are taught, if we have been instructed wisely, and it is a context in which the terminology of spiritual betrothal and spiritual marriage is not mentioned.

When, however, one becomes more concerned about the

climax of the spiritual life, he is met with the confusion of an entirely different terminology, like another train on another track. Before he can board the other train, he must apparently wait for some extraordinary, supernatural happenings called spiritual betrothal and spiritual marriage. Thus it may appear that the principles which have carried him so well and so far must now be abandoned for some new, mysterious relationship, probably unattainable by ordinary persons, and so there can arise a false segmentation of the spiritual life.

Therefore, as a result of all we have said, it seems advisable in a work which seeks to clarify and to be practical, that we not usually use expressions, which can be clarified only by careful explanation. Rather we will usually employ a synonym, that of *transforming union*, which has a more precise and universal meaning.

Transforming union not only includes the essence of what is beautifully understood of the spiritual marriage of the soul to God but, even more, it gives love a direct and impelling goal. We readily understand what union is, and even from our earliest spiritual life we have become accustomed to desire it, always more of it. We received it by grace from the beginning in our baptism. And if at the end of our spiritual life, the union becomes more vivid to us by our comprehending how deeply we are now united with God, even likened in some way to the union of marriage, we at least have in the one word "union" a single concept which covers the whole of our spiritual journey. Our train is on the same track throughout; we do not have to leave behind our baggage and change to another.

We also readily understand what it means to be transformed. Union as used here is not the union of one thing glued onto another. It is the union of likeness, the likeness of children to Father through sanctifying grace, the oneness by which the creature participates (though most remotely at best) in the divine nature. When we were baptized as children, and thus became adopted children of God, we did not have this oneness in an intense degree. Only by growing spiritually, by being so transformed that our soul becomes more and more like God, is a greater degree of oneness achieved.

Thus there is a need to be transformed if we are to become very close to God. The "old man" within us must be transformed into the likeness of the new man, Jesus Christ. The need to be transformed is understood in the figure our Lord gave us; we must be transformed into children. "Unless you turn and become like children," he told us. However, in this book we will not continuously use the term "child" but rather "transforming union" because as we have said, spiritual childhood does not in itself describe the end of the spiritual life, at least not completely. Rather, it describes what we must become in order to be led into union with God completely, but as such it does not describe the union. Nor does any other single symbol describe it either.

"Transforming union" tells us that we are transformed by union with God. This union is basically sanctifying grace but now there is a much higher degree of it, a much greater likeness to God. God reaches out in love by actual grace, drawing our soul into this union. The soul is thus transformed into the Beloved. He transforms us in uniting us; he unites us to himself in transforming us.

Even though one cannot have this union without having great love, still our loving desires do not as such transform us. They are very helpful and, with our prayers and other meritorious actions, do draw God down to us, so to speak. Yet the union is not brought about by us, even by great desire, but principally by God's actual graces and loving mercy, which make possible the degree of sanctifying grace, which implies close friendship, or if you will, which implies (and always surpasses) the closeness of marriage in the relationship of bridegroom and bride.

With no truth can the soul claim this transformation and this union *exclusively* as its own work. This impossibility is based not only on the truth that all things in the moral and spiritual life come principally because of grace, but it is also based on the soul's own experience at this time. In the earlier stages of the spiritual life the very effort which we must make to throw off bad habits, to acquire the good ones, and to direct the mind again and again to God in prayer and purity of intention, all may make it seem that spiritual progress is very much our own labor. Apparently, we might feel, all this has been largely accomplished by our own strength of will and clearness of intellect . . . but only apparently, because "Without me you can do nothing."

In the latter stages, however, there is little room for such an illusion. In the life of the virtues, more and more do we now experience that some greater power is working, greater than our own force of will and judgment.

Likewise, in the life of prayer it now may also happen that, more and more comes from God, and that less and less is there need of our own strong effort. But on the contrary, when God is not "present," the effort and its result are dismal.

One must never make the mistake of a faulty extrapolation as to the amount of actual grace required in this period as compared with the earlier periods. This is to say; if it required a certain amount of grace to cast off the vices, and acquire the virtues, one must not conclude that only the same amount is required in the latter stages—or that even a less amount is required, because there appear to be fewer obstacles to be overcome and therefore less need for strong effort.

On the contrary, the higher one goes, the more grace is needed, always more in proportion to each degree of closeness to God. This situation is like trying to push together two objects, which have been charged with the same kind of electric charge, either positive or negative. When they are close to each other, much more force is required to push them closer than when they were farther apart. It should not really surprise us that the steps of becoming closer to God, now require more grace than they did before. For, on one hand there is the infinite majesty and holiness of God, which should make it a fearsome experience for any creature to come close, and on the other hand, there is the human nature which is fallen and prone to sin.

However, despite the fact that much more grace is required now, God, the Beloved, who is also the endlessly Powerful and Bountiful, has ever more grace waiting—always more than should be necessary, for even here we are all "unprofitable servants." At this point, besides the likelihood of contemplative prayer, the gifts of the Holy Spirit are more in operation than they were previously. This is to say that we are now being propelled toward God, not so much by our own power, even with his help, but rather by his power acting with our cooperation which now largely amounts to our consent and abandonment to his grace, not however without much suffering. To say that great graces of all kinds are not operating, but that the progress becomes easier, only because mature virtues and greater experience now make things easier, would show little conception of what it means to reach out of oneself into the full embrace of the absolute and transcendent God. "Man shall not see me and live" (Ex 33:20). It is something which the most virtuous of non-spiritual people cannot even apprehend.

God's indescribably intense love for us, is adequate in providing for our weakness. All he wants is our love and willingness to cooperate in this work of our sanctification . . . and our persevering desire and prayer for it. It is he who unites and he who transforms. He unites as he transforms. He transforms as he unites. All is done by his grace, all effort is because of his love. We can be joined to him most intimately by emphasizing great love and union. It is even quite possible that high degrees of union may come about without the soul's understanding anything about it except the closeness to God which is perfect conformity to his will.

In the transforming union there are degrees of union, and this should not surprise us. There comes a time in human love when we are truly friends with another but nevertheless with a love that can always be increased. The same is true of God and the individual soul, even in the closeness of the final stage of union on earth, when we are perfect or very close to it—to the degree that any human being, while on earth, can be called perfect in the sight of God.

Later on we shall discuss various characteristics usually ascribed to the transforming union. Some of them, as we shall see, have only a limited usefulness. For, it is always difficult to assign definite spiritual phenomena to a definite period in the inner progress of the individual soul. We can waste much effort and gain much confusion if we turn from the simple path of the spiritual life as taught by the Scriptures and the Church, and individualized by the plan of the Holy Spirit for each of us. The freedom of the Holy Spirit and the intricate design of each of our uniquely different spiritual personalities, make it useless in practice to become greatly concerned whether, for instance, this be the betrothal or the spiritual marriage, or whether the Dark Night must come here or there, or precisely what kind of prayer we may be experiencing at the moment.

In practice it should be enough that we be conscious of a love for God which increasingly centers on him, his will, or his glory in a degree that can be called perfect, this rather than on the self, on others, or on other things insofar as we may be drawn from him. Then, in always wanting more and more of his love, and wanting always to give more love and the proofs of love, we must trust that interiorly we have been transformed, and are still being transformed into the likeness to God, which we can only poorly call a high degree of sanctifying grace.

One advantage of a clear idea of the later part of the spiritual life is, that those who want God very much, need not spend their lives awaiting some mysterious experience, which they can interpret as spiritual betrothal or spiritual marriage. Yet even so, we are not left without considerable confusion when we think of the apex of our lives in terms of the transforming union. Enough perplexing things have also been said about this, and as with all obscurity, we may find our spiritual life a groping after, rather than a grasping for what we clearly want and can attain by God's grace. Thus there will be a slowing of momentum toward the ultimate union we can have with God on earth.

Part of the difficulty arises, as in the case of spiritual marriage, because of language. In the spiritual life, and perhaps even more as we look toward the final stages of the spiritual life, we try to receive direction from the words of those who have successfully passed through before us. But successful though they were in the passage, their descriptions are likely to be less so. They are describing what to them is most certain and real, but they must put it into language that is human, and has only an analogical or metaphorical relationship with the reality. Thus their language is often that of the senses, filled with the images of things that we see, hear, touch, and feel. But the original experience was most often something beyond the senses. No doubt to themselves, who speak in the bright light of the experience, the language is clear. To us, however, who are trying to look from their words back into the experience, it is not clear. To solve our difficulties, we must use what is certain to us. We must interpret the language in the clear light of the principles of the faith and of right reason. No matter how exalted the experience, it can never exceed what we know by faith, nor be contrary to it, or to what we know by reason enlightened by faith.

We can see this difficulty of language in two passages from writers who need no defense in regard to Catholic orthodoxy. St. Teresa of Avila says of the seventh mansion: "Here it is like water descending from heaven into a river or spring, where one is so mixed with the other, that it cannot be discerned which is the river water and which the rain water" (*Interior Castle*, 7th Mansion, Ch. 2). Nor is St. John of the Cross free from the same ambiguity, even when he does not use metaphors. In a stanza of *The Dark Night of the Soul*, upon which he never found time to comment, he says with unequaled beauty:

> "O night that guided me,
> O night more lovely than the dawn,
> O night that joined Beloved with the lover.
> Lover transformed into the Beloved."

It is this last line which could cause us trouble if we did not know the orthodoxy of this great teacher in the Church. But others who have experienced God, and who have also written and spoken, have not escaped the trap that seems to lie in the path of the mystics, the taint of pantheism, the unfortunate language that suggests that the creature becomes so much one with the deity, that its nature is completely absorbed.

Theologically we can account for the language, if we make a distinction always made by the authentic Catholic mystics. We are divine indeed, not by becoming God, but by participation. The manner of this participation is mysterious and defies complete explanation, but the participation or sharing is there: "He has granted us the very great and precious promises, so that through them you may become partakers of the divine nature" (2 P 1:4). This participation, as we have already said, is sanctifying grace, and it is no exclusive property of those in the unitive way. Yet it has degrees, and we can have any great degree of it without being aware of it, for grace as such is not something apprehensible by the senses or by reason. But to some of those who have attained a high degree of it, God has shown their state by the embrace of his love in what we would call higher contemplative prayer. So overwhelming is this experience that they can easily be excused for not using precise theological language.

If we use a comparison taken from St. John of the Cross, we will see how this confusion can arise in practice. "This divine light acts upon the soul, which it is purging and preparing for union with it, in the same way as fire acts upon a log of wood, in order to transform it into itself" (*Dark Night of the Soul*, bk. II. ch. 10). If we look upon fire as St. John of the Cross did, as a separate entity (indeed as one of the four elements constituting the whole material nature), we will understand the full import of the image.

The log first becomes warm, and then glows because of the flame. The flame is in it and all around it. It is so filled with the flame, that its very life seems to be the flame. Indeed if the log had consciousness, it could be conscious of nothing but the heat and the flame of which it seems to be a part. Can we not say then that in this union of love between God and soul the impression caused by the glimpse of what God is, and what his love is, becomes so overwhelming that man can experience nothing else at the time? He cannot even reflect on his own identity or on the fact that it is he who is experiencing this delight. He is completely aware of the Other. And yet it is the "I" who is experiencing, who feels the delight, and, even if not reflecting, knows the Other in the union.

The "I" is the wood, not the fire; it is of earth and not the flame. It has its own properties of weight and substance, as St. John of the Cross notes well according to the science of his times (and which serves us equally well as our own for these purposes). The properties which make up the self are always the self, very much the limited creature of God, which cannot be absorbed by even temporary annihilation into the completely transcendent being, uncreated and unlimited. But how difficult, how almost impossible in poor human words to tell us all this afterwards.

Perhaps we can explain how this happens. God is a being so infinitely beyond our capacity to comprehend him that any very intense closeness to him, would so fill the soul, that it would be unable to comprehend clearly. Even an intense, merely human experience, such as extreme fear or joy, can leave the mind in a state of shock. Thus the soul in close union with God, can easily feel a oneness which it could not humanly be expected to comprehend and later relate with fine theological distinction.

The impression of oneness cannot help but follow from God's way of loving. God, in a sense can love nothing but himself. That is, he can love only what is good, and good is always a reflection of himself. When something does not reflect him in some way, it is to that extent evil. He cannot love evil but only loves good, loves therefore himself in the sense that he loves all good because of its relationship to himself.

The soul of man reflects or manifests God more than all the glories of the physical world, for herein is especially contained the image and likeness of God, in which our nature was created. An immeasurably greater likeness, however, is possessed by the soul in sanctifying grace, now not merely an image, but having a participation in the divine nature itself. The love which God bears this soul is also basically a love of himself, but here is a love of his goodness now reflected in the highest manner that we can conceive, outside of the hypostatic union in Christ.

As we grow in sanctifying grace, our likeness to God increases and our love for him increases in the same measure. This love, of course, bears a likeness to the nature of God for, "God is love" (1 Jn 4:16), but it also has a likeness to the way he lives. God lives a life of infinite love in the Blessed Trinity. Thus, in the love of the transforming union, our way of living has a special likeness to God. But besides this, love brings with itself an even greater oneness; it impels toward the other, we toward God, and God toward us. It is evident then, for all these reasons, that when we have a high degree of sanctifying grace and love, we also have oneness with God in a high degree. This oneness arising from likeness is what the mystic sees.

This brings us to consider further God's way of loving. God's love is not only himself but it is one complete, eternal act, comprising at once the love of the Blessed Trinity within itself and the love of himself in his likeness in all the good of creation. This likeness, love and consequent oneness impresses itself overpoweringly on the mind of the mystic. The impression is magnificently vivid, not as a reasoned theological proposition as we have given it here, but in the blinding light of experience. His human mind grasps all this essentially but indiscriminately, like a man suddenly coming from a dark room into the sunlight. It comprehends the oneness arising from God and from the likeness to God in the soul. It also comprehends the oneness of God's love with the soul's own love. The impression that its overwhelmed mind receives, can only cry out in expressions like: "I being absorbed in Thy beauty." This when explained becomes: "Thus I shall see Thee in Thy beauty and Thou shalt see me in Thy beauty; and I shall see myself in Thee in Thy beauty; and Thou shalt see Thyself in me in Thy beauty" (*Spiritual Canticle*, XXXVI, 5). There is always the irreducible "I" which bears the likeness and receives the love.

Besides, no matter how close the identity this union may seem to be, it is immeasurably less than two other unions which nevertheless necessarily involve distinctness: the distinctness of the three Persons in the Blessed Trinity, and the distinctness of the two natures in the hypostatic union of the God-man, Christ.

Even love, crying as it does for union, cannot bring about identity. The unlikenesses between God and ourselves are always infinitely greater than the likenesses. The highest degree of transformation of which any created nature is capable, will always leave it infinitely different from him. As a poor example, in mathematics the calculating of certain relationships brings one line on a graph always closer to another, but no matter how much and how long we might calculate, the two lines will never touch. Transforming union only makes us more godlike, but never God.

Another example may also help. We can compare the soul to a

tall tree, and God to the sun. The tree grows up reaching for the sun. It is enormously closer to the sun in comparison with a seedling on the ground, but it will never reach the sun. The laws of its own nature, the distance, and the physical conditions of outer space will always leave it most remote from the sun, much though it lives for and loves its light and warmth.

These two examples explain the truth better when taken together. The line, which is the loving soul, draws ever closer, so that no human eye can distinguish it from the other line, which is God, the Beloved. Thus the soul at that closeness intimately experiences the love, power, and majesty of the infinite God. But looking at the nature of the soul as compared to God's nature, we see that it remains like the tree, an impossible distance away, always a human soul, always a limited and dependent creature.

The transforming union involves nothing different in kind, but only in degree. It is fundamentally based on the same sanctifying grace and love with which we are so familiar, and only requires a higher degree. We can therefore, accept the fact that the transforming union is not so mysterious as we might have thought. With an essential part of our uncertainty taken away, many of us may find the hope that this union is not, by its nature, denied to anyone and we may also receive the courage to seek it.

Chapter 4

UNION AND TRANSFORMATION
THROUGH LOVE

Union is the instinctive direction taken by love, and love under the influence of actual grace will continually transform us until we reach the closest union. In reference to God, union indicates limitless possibility; a deeper and closer union can always be given. Although this oneness can never become identity with God, greater union in this life can always bring greater depths and absorption into the flame that is the love of the Beloved, the flame that is the Beloved.

Union in its perfection can only come about by love, and love acts to break down the barriers between the soul and God. We have already mentioned that more grace is required in these last steps than was needed previously. This would seem to indicate that the progress now is proportionately slower. But not so, or at least not necessarily nor always.

As we grow closer to God, sanctifying grace is increased and along with it the deeply rooted, habitual love in the soul. Greater love means greater yearning for the Beloved, and since God's love always outmatches our own he gives an abundance of actual grace for closer union. Actual grace here is the impelling action of the Holy Spirit in our souls, moving us toward transforming union at an accelerated rate, as a stone falls to earth at an ever-increasing speed. St. John of the Cross indicates that, once the processes of close union have begun, the ultimate earthly union can come in a short time: "God quickly transforms the soul into himself" (*Spiritual Canticle*, XX, 4). And yet there is always possible a closer degree of this union, as the saint himself discovered (See *Living Flame of Love* Int., 3).

This growing union is not unlike some of our human loves. Acquaintance can deepen into interest, then into remote friendship, and remain that way for some time. But once a certain threshold has been crossed, the love between friends can increase at an enormous rate. Similarly, but much more, souls in that divine fire "are moved by love to greater love of God" (*Spiritual Canticle*, XXIV, 7).

Love, therefore, is the principal personal force which will unite us to God, as well as transform us into God-likeness. If we need proof, the gift of love which he has spread throughout the world should be proof enough, proof not by reasoning, but by merely observing that oneness of heart is the effect of love. And from union of the heart comes union of life, purpose, and ideals. When love unites, it transforms, ideally always for the better.

We want union because we want the beloved as beloved. Even in the highest of human loves, we instinctively want the beloved in some way, for our own, and it would be foolishness to say otherwise. But much more than this legitimate love of the other because of the self, we want the good of the beloved. Yet we still never lose the desire, so long as we love, that the good of the other may somehow include ourselves, as part and in high degree.

Such close and intense union can come, only when certain barriers of separateness are broken down. If the human love is also good, we become transformed (while still remaining ourselves) into something better; in many ways we become different in the practical details of life, and in our psychological and spiritual orientation. Thus experience of our own nature is an accurate teacher about love, where our reason can only crudely analyze. And so it is a truism needing no demonstration that it is principally love which will bring us to the closest union with God, and will transform us into a likeness of Christ.

If we wish to use our reason about love, we can easily demonstrate this push of love toward union, if we consider the spiritual life under the aspect of perfection. Perfection, in Christian teaching, does not ultimately have a self-centered terminus. Like all perfection, it implies a fittingness or correspondence to a model, or better, to an end or purpose. A perfect clock, for instance, has little to do with the design of the casing but everything to do with keeping accurate time. Our basic purpose on earth and in heaven, is union with God, and this union must be primarily a union of wills. A union of intellects, as expressed in knowledge alone, could leave us far from him, as indeed it has left the devils. Union of wills is accomplished principally through love. Indeed all the acts of the will, in one way or another, are ultimately acts of love.

Love is the golden thread used in the weaving of our spiritual life from the beginning to the end. But it does not always appear in the same pattern. St. Thomas (*Summa Theologica*: II, II; 24; 9) profoundly distinguishes a difference. In the early stages, love primarily impels a man to remove the great obstacles which may stand in the way of this love. This is the principal work of this first period, even though a man would be mistaken if he acted only negatively. For he must also acquire the virtues which are the fitness for greater love, and reach out for the union of friendship with God. Indeed if close friendship is his primary *motive*, he will do much better in rooting out the vices found in this early period, and much better also in growing in the virtues, which is the primary *work* of love during the second or illuminative stage. But in this final period about which we are speaking, love takes on the principal aspect of union with God, and, if granted, the enjoyment of God. Love, always capable of increase, now has the principal aim of greater oneness with the beloved God.

This union is the ultimate of spiritual and human perfection, and implies the total and complete giving of ourselves to God. Perhaps we had thought we did this in our first fervor, and also many times along the way, but then we found out that it was more difficult to give totally than we thought, especially when our need of purification became more apparent. But again we may have thought that the giving was total when we had disciplined ourselves into the fully Christian man, except that there may still have been the dark creatures of the unconscious, those attitudes of rebellion and resistance of our deformed nature, which hitherto had defied conversion by hiding in the darkness. It is only

after all these contradictions are settled, whether through the
Dark Night, or in other ways (but always by God's grace, since the
healing must go too deep for our own efforts) that it is possible for
us to have the oneness of mind and will with God which is implied
in total giving.

Before that we give all only in our desire to give all. We give
love, service, worship, obedience, but not the whole of man. But in
the state of spiritual perfection, the whole of man is given by being
united with the whole that is God. Life now is the Beloved.

We must here again note certain expressions of love, which
come to us from the mystics and which are possible of a less than
accurate understanding. Sometimes we read about an equality of
love between God and ourselves. A writer like St. John of the
Cross always carefully distinguishes the unmeasurable difference
between the powers of God and creature, but the idea is used out
of context often enough to merit explanation.

When we speak of love as it is in God, we understand that
God's love is, in many ways different from our own. God's love is
himself, and therefore it is infinite as is his nature, infinite as are
all the other attributes of his nature, such as his wisdom and
power. They are all one in the absolute unity and simplicity of that
nature, limitless and unchanging.

Our own love is necessarily limited, just as we ourselves are
necessarily limited, just because we are creatures. This necessary
limitation has nothing to do with any voluntary imperfection on
our part, and it is not even the result of original sin. It is the basic
reality of all creation. God simply cannot make a creature capable
of any infinite actuality or potentiality. Not even the best of us, not
even the human Christ, nor the Blessed Virgin, can fulfill the
totality of something that is infinite. We, as limited creatures, can
do and receive, only according to some degree or measure. Only
God himself can fulfill the infinity of God, and this is done only in
the infinite and mysterious love that the Father has for the Son
and the Son for the Father, which love proceeds from both as the
Third Person in the Blessed Trinity. All creatures must fall infinitely below such a fulfillment of the infinite.(See St. Thomas: II,

II; 24;8 and 184;2. Also St. Francis de Sales, *Treatise on the Love of God*: bk. 3, ch. 1)

There is, however, a broad sense in which we can speak of equality of love between God and ourselves. Every soul was destined to give all of what it is, to give to God all the love of which it is capable. Some have been made capable of giving more, others of giving less. Yet even the lowliest soul ought to give all, ought to embrace the divine will, with its full capacity. God then can receive an essentially total giving from every creature, whether the giving be greater or less, because each gives all that it can give. Thus, just as on one hand, God's love is all of himself, so also on the other hand, we can give all of the love of which we are capable. In this there is a certain sense of equality: our all of love given to the All of Love.

In general the impression of equality with God comes to the mystics because of what they are made to feel by God. Love, in the sense of friendship, tends to make equals. God treats the beloved soul *as if* it were equal. But of course, it is not really equal, any more than St. John and St. Mary Magdalen were equal to Christ.

Perhaps this can be clarified by an example. Let us suppose that the Holy Father had a friend for many years before he became pope. Now even though he is pope, he still treats the friend in private as an equal, opening his heart to the friend, and accepting all that the friend says to him. But even so, the inequality between the two would still be enormous, although on these occasions the friend is not conscious of the difference. Nor is the soul in this state always conscious of the inequality when it meets God in love. St. John of the Cross says, "The fruit and the operation of love, grow in this state to such an extent that they become very much those of the life to come; so much so that *to the soul it appears that they are so* and it ventures to use these words *which one ventures to use only of the next life*." (*Living Flame of Love*, I, 14. Emphasis added.)

So far we have been speaking of love as the attribute of God, to which there can be no real equality. When we consider the actual love between God and ourselves, we must distinguish the love that we have on the way, and the love we will have in heaven. St. John of the Cross has this to say on it: "Notwithstanding the transformation which the soul is experiencing in this life, all the vastness of her love cannot succeed in equaling the perfection of love, whereby she is loved by God." However, in heaven it will be different: "Therefore she desires the clear transformation of glory, wherein she will succeed in equaling the said love" (*Spiritual Canticle*, XXXVIII, 3). A few words of explanation will show how our state in heaven will bring about an equality in our actual love for God.

God's eternal will is unchangeable. He is "the Father of lights, with whom there is no variation or shadow due to change" (Jm 1:17). On earth it is we who change in respect to him. Thus our love for him here is something which can and does change, but in eternity it will be unchangeable, because there the human will is unchangeable. The degree of our love must forever remain as it is seen in the depths of our soul when we leave this life.

However, this degree of love must be understood in the changed circumstances of heaven, as compared to earth. When we say that our degree of love (corresponding as it does to our degree of sanctifying grace) will forever remain the same, we do not mean that the *condition* of this love is the same as that on earth. Indeed in some men this would mean a rather dismal heaven, because they love God so little in this life, as would be the case of a great sinner who repents with just enough contrition to have his sins forgiven on his death bed. In heaven however the weak condition of this man's love is transformed, as indeed will be the love of those who on earth loved God in the highest degrees. As St. Thomas tells us, "the gifts of God always exceed our merits" (*Comm. in Mt*, ch. 5). For all of us, our love will be transformed into a glowing or burning fire, when by the light of glory we will be able to see God as he really is. Thus, his eternal reward of love will be, in a true sense, more than we have brought with us; in return for our love on earth it will be "good measure, pressed down and shaken together, running over" (Lk 6:38). It will be in proportion to the amount of habitual love with which we left this earth. And since we can no longer merit in heaven, it will stay in that proportion forever.

In heaven each of us will have an individual relationship to the infinite immensity that is God's love. Of that unchangeable infinity we attract from it, so to speak, only that degree of love which we bring. It is God's love indeed, and we will be blessedly aware that it is an infinitely superior kind than our own. But the unchangeableness of God prevents our receiving more actual love from him than we are able to draw out from this infinite love by our own fixed degree of love.

It is like a large stove in the middle of a room. Let us say that it is unchangeable in its position and the amount of heat given off. The people in the room will be heated according to their closeness to the stove, and their position is fixed forever. In the same manner our relationship in love of God is fixed by his judgment, a judgment begun in eternity and confirmed by his knowledge of our final degree of love on earth. In our perfect conformity to his will we joyfully embrace our degree of love, now supremely content in that it is equal to the love he has chosen to give us and with which he will love us for all eternity.

This is one reason why heaven will be an endless delight for us. There we will come to love God with the equality that true love always wants to give the other. Unlike some of the loves of this world, God's love for us will never be less than what we give to him. Despite the equality of love between us, it is not the same as the love of two human beings. God's love is always himself, eternally able to delight us, by simply being what he is.

Along similar lines, it is also sometimes said that in the transforming union, we love God to the full extent that he deserves to be loved. This is of course impossible in any absolute meaning, for God is infinitely lovable. He can be loved as he deserves to be loved, as we have just said, only as the Father and the Son love in the Holy Trinity, and which love comes forth as the infinite love which is the Holy Spirit, infinite in the same nature as are the other two Divine Persons. No finite love, not even that of the human will of Christ, is capable of that. We can only love God to the extent that he can be loved by a human will. We would wish to give him more, even the infinite love of the Trinity within itself, and in this unfulfillable desire, there can be some truth in the saying that, we love him as he deserves to be loved.

In this desire we can offer to him something more than we are capable of offering from ourselves. We offer him back a most precious gift he has given to us, the Spirit of Love, the Holy Spirit. He is God's uncreated gift to us. "The love of God has been poured into our hearts through the Holy Spirit, who was given to us" (Rm 5:5). Thus, although we by ourselves cannot offer more than anything finite, we can offer back what is infinite, the eternal love of the Holy Spirit, who dwells within us. As far as we can, we make this to be our love so that God may in some remote sense be loved by us as he deserves to be loved absolutely. St. Thérèse has put this more simply and directly: "To love Thee as Thou lovest me, I must borrow Thy own love—thus only can my desire be satisfied." But this is not the same as saying that we by ourselves can give to God any actual love which would equal his attribute of being infinitely lovable.

In practice, for the most part we ought not express love to God in this way, as if through another's love. This would not allow us to be ourselves, the same selves by whom God wants to be loved. We must love God in our own way as it is given to us at the moment. Only by actual desire, expressed when we are moved to express it, and by implicit desire at all times, will we make his love to be ours.

Indeed, it is the Holy Spirit who is working in us silently and hiddenly, to enable us to give any love. In these final stages of the spiritual life his operation is more involved in our love, as it is in so much else, and our own faculties now often move less consciously and deliberately. In such oneness with his operation, our merit lies in the fact that we freely consent to His working, even though we may not be directly conscious that it is he who is working. But in this way, our love comes to have a certain completeness of perfection. Just as we are to be perfect in our own order of things, as God is perfect in his, so our love for him becomes a complete and perfectly fulfilled flame permeating us, just as his own love is an infinite attribute permeating him.

In these chapters we have been examining the language of those who have experienced God, in ways that are beyond adequate expression in words. Perhaps it may seem that in reducing the ecstatic to the sober language of familiar reality, we have taken away their power to inspire. But not so. The mystics are still there to be read, and their inspiration should have a deeper effect because of a clearer understanding.

Inspiration needs a basis of personal reality, before it can become an effective hope. In reading the words of St. Thérèse of Lisieux, for instance, we do not observe any great inspiration drawn from the splendid writings of her namesake, Teresa of Avila. On the contrary what a discouragement it would have been for her, if she could look for guidance only in the descriptions of the sixth and seventh mansions of St. Teresa. But at some time in her life, she saw the way God was drawing her, and understood that she would never be taking the same steps as her spiritual mother. Also through the clear teaching of the Scriptures, through her intelligent reading of St. John of the Cross, and surely also by an interior instinct of the Holy Spirit she knew much more: that great love of God, an absolute desire to please him in the details of her life, and complete abandonment to his will would infallibly bring her close to him. For her that was what sanctity meant, and it must also be so for us, sanctity put in an understandable and, with the grace of God, humanly possible context.

Thus we do not have to spend our lives unconsciously looking for the ecstasies which, some seem to tell us, ought to precede the transforming union or spiritual marriage. We can put our hand in God's and look to Him for our way into his heart. The problem of great sanctity for ourselves becomes a simple one, nothing different from what we learned at first but much more intense: love, trust, dependence, diligence. It is the steadily increasing absorption of ourselves into the ways of God and his eventual total penetration of our lives . . . and also, if this is his way for us, an ever increasing awareness of actual, conscious communion in this perfect friendship.

Chapter 5

THE ESSENCE OF THE TRANSFORMING UNION

The unitive way is often explained, as we have said, as if there were two different trains traveling in the same direction, but on different tracks. On the one track we are carried forward by the various virtues, and then suddenly we must change to another train. On this track we are guided by descriptions of experiences which are often purely personal, but which are emphasized as if they were the way that all must follow in order to ride this train.

If we wish to discover the essence of the transforming union, we must separate the personal phenomena from those which are general, and this is not particularly difficult. In her seventh mansion, St. Teresa mentions certain impressions of the Sacred Humanity, and of the Blessed Trinity. That these were personal gifts to this extraordinarily gifted woman, seems clear. For on the other hand, when St. John of the Cross speaks of the spiritual marriage, he does not require anything which transcends the order of sanctifying grace, marvelous though grace is in itself (See *Spiritual Canticle*, XXII). The task of reaching the essence of this state is not hereby finished.

There is no doubt that some of those who have written from their own experience on this summit of the spiritual life, have given us descriptions which, even if we eliminate the extraordinary and the personal, leave us in no doubt that they were in contact with God in a most intimate way. But are these the only people who have reached the transforming union? Obviously not. Not all who have reached this state have written about their experiences, not all have been canonized, nor even have been recognized by their contemporaries. The problem then, becomes the finer distinction between what may happen often and what is of the essence, that is, what is always present in the transforming union in order for it to be the transforming union.

The essence of a thing must be described by something that is held by all in that state, and not held by others who are not in that state. In what, then, must this union basically consist? Into what must all be transformed? Beyond a doubt, we must all be transformed into Christ, into the fullness of Christ, insofar as fallen nature can be transformed into him. And if we are not transformed into him, all the phenomena of the later mystical life would be either an extraordinary help given to a relatively weak person or, more probably, an illusion. The more we are transformed into Christ, the closer is our union with God. But only the real and close union with God in sanctifying grace and the virtues can bring about this transformation. Transformation in this sense means aquiring a heroic degree of all the virtues, especially that of love of God and neighbor. This is the clear teaching of the gospels.

The way of the gospels is the way of following Christ, and we do this by denying ourselves, taking up our cross, keeping the commandments (especially the two great ones), and by observing at least the spirit of the counsels, such as poverty, chastity, and obedience, according to our vocation in life. In the gospels, there is nothing of spiritual betrothals and spiritual marriages, no description of the states of prayer or the dark nights. This absence of course does not invalidate these experiences, but on the other hand the fact that it was in the power of God to have delivered the gospel of perfection in these terms, but that he did not, indicates where the emphasis of our lives should be.

Mysticism is not a synonym for the transforming union. Although mysticism has many meanings which we do not want to use here, for us and in practice the mystic can be identified by the gift of infused contemplative prayer. In general this prayer is given only to those who have gone through enough purification to be relatively solid in the virtues, but it may be given by way of exception to some who are only beginners. Far more important for the essence of the transforming union, however, is the fact that not everyone in this union has had contemplative prayer in the high degree and in the relatively continuous experience, of those great saints who have written about it.

Just as we have no way of knowing how many people have contemplative prayer, so also we cannot know how many people have attained the heroic degree of the virtues, and who still do not have the intense experience of God, often described as constituting the transforming union. Theoretically it is possible that there are some who have not had contemplative prayer at all, because God can do what he wills and how he wills it. He has not promised contemplative prayer to those who seek him. In practice, moreover, we know that there were some saints whose lives had very little of any kind of contemplative prayer. Since there is both the possibility of the free choice of God, and the fact of these saints, we must seek the essence of transforming union, in something independent of the states of prayer, while still not eliminating contemplative prayer because, more than likely, it will form some part of this union, according as God calls the individual.

In forming our own mind on these matters, we can do no better than to accept the mind of the Church as shown by her procedure in beatification and canonization. In the selection and confirmation of those of us who can be used as models of sanctity for the rest of us, she does not require proof of any kind of contemplative prayer, much less of the extraordinary, such as visions, prophecies, or miracles performed during life. Instead, the major work of the process is to investigate the presence of heroic virtue, especially as evidenced by the fulfillment of the duties of our state in life.

Therefore we would place the essence of the transforming union in the high degree of sanctifying grace indicated by the heroic degree of the virtues especially love of God and neighbor. But since we cannot see sanctifying grace, for the practical purposes of establishing a goal, and of encouraging effort, we must say that the essential element of this union, in the sense of an essential sign, is the heroic degree of the virtues. By them alone, and especially by love, are we transformed into Christ and absorbingly united to God in sanctifying grace, always under the influence of the constantly necessary and even great actual graces from God. Thus, our train stays on the same track we started on, only now we may be moving faster and the scenery may be different.

Since the essence of transforming union is found in the heroic degree of the virtues, it will be necessary to understand what is meant by this degree. Heroic virtue is not just anything that is hard. Penances, for instance, that are extreme to the point of extinction, cannot be considered as virtue. Nor is it always something which goes against the desires and aspirations of human nature. Heroic virtue is determined first of all by its end or purpose, and this purpose is to make us like Christ, and to join us to God. In this it is no different from ordinary virtue, except that it is more deeply rooted and more capable of exercise under difficult conditions, where men with virtues of an ordinary degree would probably fail. It also reaches out to more extensive areas of operation either in actual fact, or in the readiness to follow ever more closely, the perfect virtues of Christ. The man of heroic virtue stands firm, (or acts, as the case might be) where others look away, perhaps finding excuses, rationalizing, or unconsciously blinding themselves to their obligations.

In practice there are indications by which we can distinguish the heroic degree from the ordinary degree. Later we shall speak of some of the virtues in particular, but in general a virtue is heroic when it is above the ordinary strength of men, even in the supernatural order. Likewise it ought not to be an isolated act; rather the proof lies in the ability to perform many acts of high degree. The "many," of course, is limited by the number of occasions offered. There is, for instance a limit upon the number of times a person can be martyred. These acts will usually be performed with promptness, ease, and even pleasure or joy, but the memory of our Lord in the Garden cautions us from stressing this too demandingly. (From the way "holy joy" is emphasized by some, it would appear that Christ himself would have difficulty in getting canonized.) Ordinarily these virtues will have been in evidence for some relatively long time. Length of time gives an indication of the intensity of the union with God, in love and in grace.

Heroic virtue becomes heroic principally through love of God. Love of God in the heroic degree is at the heart of the transforming union. In the early Church, men with such virtues came to be honored, because virtue in this degree was considered to be equivalent to martyrdom, so much does a man have to give of himself in order to achieve them.

The virtues in the heroic degree indicate the transformation that unites us in the closest friendship with God, but this does not mean that they are free from false imitation. Outwardly, all the acts of these virtues, singly taken, can be counterfeited. Thus outwardly a man can be extremely meek and humble, or notoriously charitable. Even inwardly, he might earnestly strive for heroic virtue in a compulsive desire for self-development.

The drive toward this illusion does not always have to be conscious; a man may sincerely think he is very spiritual. Perhaps he feels some failure in other areas, and he is determined to excel in this. Or perhaps his surroundings make this kind of excellence a psychological imperative if he is to maintain his neurotic form of self-respect. Long periods of prayer, with excursions into the extraordinary spiritual phenomena and into excessive penances, may also be the companions of his self-imposed virtues.

Self-centered ambition, even when unconscious, cannot deceive others unless they are ignorant of true virtue or are otherwise disposed to deception. In the first place such counterfeit virtues should show their adequacy because, although copied after real models, they show the crude hand of the copyist. Such a man cannot have an adequate and accurate idea of true virtue, but will in some way, project his pride image or neurosis instead. There will always be the element of conspicuousness about his actions because, after all, they are done with an eye for an audience which, of course, is primarily himself. There will also be lapses of virtue in the form of extremes and in the omission of those virtues which are not high on his personal list of those to be displayed. He will fail particularly in holy prudence, this noticeably in dealing with others to whom he gives spiritual advice.

We must have all the virtues in a high degree in order to have any in a high degree, all at least in willingness of mind, even when it is impossible to exercise some of them here and now. A man, for instance, who has nothing himself, cannot be liberal to the poor. Even though a man may appear to excel in one virtue, because of a special grace of God for this occasion or, because of his particular bent or training, all the rest of the virtues must with certainty be found to be present in a high degree, in order to have heroic virtue. They are not presumed to be there because of the evidence of one virtue.

Although it is not always difficult to distinguish true from false virtue in another, it is notably harder to do so in oneself. This should not surprise us, because our fitness for salvation itself is ordinarily more a matter of trust than of absolute certainty. To what extent our virtuous conduct is motivated by a secret pride image, and how much by a laudable desire for perfection principally for love of God, in short, to what extent we live for God, is difficult to discern. We can only open ourselves to God, plead much for him to make his truth incarnate in us at any cost to us, and then in trust keep on with our best efforts and our best love. But this obvious and unavoidable difficulty of inner discernment does not destroy the truth and usefulness of the heroic virtues as the essential sign of the transforming union.

Heroic virtue as the visible essence of sanctity makes the transforming union seem more attainable to everyone. Growth in the virtues is something toward which we can give all our strength, and we know that the essential element in the growth, the grace of God, is always there for the next height or degree to be reached. How different from being told that this union is only possible when God gives some mysterious and seemingly unattainable indication to the soul.

There may be on the other hand a sense of disappointment about the transforming union, because of the ordinariness of defining it in terms of the virtues, even virtues in the heroic degree. One of the appeals of the metaphors used by the mystics, lies in the escape from the ordinariness of this world into one of love, joy, and communion with the Beloved. Therefore, it is important to remember that the heroic degree of the virtues, is by no means a complete description of the state of perfection. For a given individual the transforming union may be all that the mystics have described, or rather it may be what they keep telling us cannot be described. But for those whom God may be calling to perfection more by the way of faith, it would be a deception to promise what will not be given, and what they will foresee very little possibility of attaining. It would be a deception which could end by discouraging them completely. The sober truth of the heroic degree of the virtues not only tells what all must attain, even the most gifted of the true mystics, but also gives others hope which God will not leave unfulfilled.

Despite the apparent ordinariness, however, the life of one in the heroic degree of the virtues can truly be called divine (that is, the life of God) divine though known only by faith instead of by the light of mystical experience. For, most basic of all, there is the close union of sanctifying grace. Through this adoption by God, we become like him in such a manner as to be called sons, thereby also sharing somehow in his own divine nature. As perfect men and women we will have this divineness in a high degree.

Our manner of living is divine also; we actually *live* the life of God. By the heroic degree of the virtues, and by the increasing light, strength and guidance of the Holy Spirit, God's will is constantly being fulfilled in our attitudes and our actions, despite our consciousness of weakness and poverty without him. As St. Francis de Sales tells us, "A soul in love with God is so transformed as to become identified with the will of God, instead of being merely obedient to it."

An example which far surpasses our own possibilities may help to understand this. What the hypostatic union meant to the human nature of Christ, that his life and actions are thus made divine, similarly, though in a very different and in a much lesser sense, does our life become divine through this union. Also, as the life of God himself is a life of love in the Three Divine Persons, so our life is centered on him in an intense and constant love, at least in the intention of the will which shows itself through our virtues.

Thus even those whose way to perfection is principally traveled in faith, can say of themselves the same words as did St. John of the Cross, who in the end lived in the light: "The soul lives the life of God. For in this soul is fulfilled that which St. Paul says: 'It is no longer I who live, but Christ who lives in me'" (*Spiritual Canticle* XXXIII, 5; Gal 2:20).

Chapter 6

"BE PERFECT"

It might be objected that, in naming the heroic degree of the virtues as the visible sign of spiritual perfection, we have strayed a long way from the simple concept of the child, as given by Christ in the gospels, but not so. We must repeat, in the first place, that the God-given symbol of the child is intended principally to indicate the way to arrive at spiritual perfection, but does not fully describe it. The two concepts, however, are even closer than this. The truth is that no one will ever acquire the heroic degree of all the virtues, unless he is a child. Especially is this true in the last stages of the spiritual life, when increase in the virtues is no longer so much acquired by our own efforts as by being given. As children in the spirit we will receive greatly from God, because we depend very little on ourselves.

The child's dependence is therefore an absolute necessity for the heroic degree of the virtues, but some people will also find a personal reason for keeping the attitude of the child before them. Many of us are distracted from looking at God and from wanting God, because we look at ourselves too much. We seem to want perfection for ourselves almost more than we want God. This is a danger in proposing a tangible goal, such as heroic virtue; it can be worked for, in some sense it must always be worked for. But worked for or given, it can become something we glory in, with only a perfunctory reference to God. But the ideal child is by nature ingenuous, and is not self-admiring.

The soul will usually be aware of its great progress at this point. But it does not rest on these gifts. They are always and deeply seen as coming from God, and the unworthiness of this same soul is likewise very clear. No one ever arrived at the heroic degree of all the virtues by deciding to build a perfect man. It comes only by looking at God more than at oneself. It comes only by loving God and wanting him, both of these very much.

In the rest of this chapter we are going to discuss two things: one, certain clarifications concerning spiritual perfection, and two, some of the conditions for the journey, that is, the routing of it, because the journey does not consist only in the end, but also in many details on the way.

As to the first, so completely in control are the virtues of a person in the transforming union, that this state is not falsely compared to that of original justice, the state of Adam and Eve before the Fall. Yet we must not exaggerate the degree of perfection required. Heroic virtue does not necessarily mean absolute perfection or sinlessness. Although the transforming union is a prelude to our entrance into heaven, it is not the fullness of perfection we will have there. The saints were unanimous in affirming their imperfection, and we have St. Paul to head the list: "Not that I have already obtained this (the resurrection from the dead) or am already perfect" (Ph 3:12). And although St. Teresa of Avila and St. John of the Cross seem to disagree as to whether a man in this state may sin, the practice of the Church in canonizations is to disregard even deliberate venial sin, by those who have attained the heroic degree of the virtues, provided that due sorrow was expressed, satisfaction made, and steps taken to avoid a similar fall in the future.

The feeling of security from sin, which some have experienced, and written about, may arise from the great trust inspired by the security of God's presence felt in unitive prayer; in such a state, it would seem impossible ever to sin again. But still the fact of sinlessness is enough in evidence for us to expect it to be a normal characteristic of the transforming union. Although not all are united to God in the same degree, (for there are degrees in this union just as there are degrees of union in human marriages), surely the great love for God and his corresponding love expressed in actual grace and in protection from occasions of sin, will quite universally keep us from all sins, except perhaps those of partial inadvertence, and even these will become very few.

So disciplined is the whole man and so filled with basic love of God and the desire to please him, that even the tendencies to sin will have disappeared in practice, except perhaps in circumstances where temptation of one kind or another is allowed so that we may merit more love from God, expiate for sins of others if not for our own, or win graces for others in particular, for the Church, or for the world. These temptations may also be permitted to keep us humble; great care must be taken by God to keep us at the high intensity of friendship. In our own tendency to level off or even go downward, we will recognize deeply that our sanctification is his work and not our own. Now, however, we become more responsive to him even in our weakness.

Yet even the weakest of us is made strong in the virtues by the grace of God. So strong now are these habits of thinking, willing and acting, that the influence of the devil is correspondingly weakened. Much emphasis is sometimes placed on this, and not without reason. St. Teresa of Avila, after having been at one time a lax nun, came to know the devil as a coward. The virtues become a wall which he cannot penetrate. Also God and his angels cause many of the devil's best laid plans to turn back on him to his own confusion. Therefore, so we are assured, he flees from all contact with the soul.

Despite the great stress placed on this, however, in practice we cannot be that sure of it. Purity of soul did not prevent the devil from coming close to Christ. St. Luke tells us that after the temptation in the desert, "the devil departed from him until an opportune time" (Lk 4:13), perhaps most significantly in the garden and on the cross. St. Paul was given "a thorn in the flesh, a messenger of Satan to harass me" (2 Cor 12:7). St. Thérèse of Lisieux suffered much from him during her final months.

Like many of the characteristics often listed for the transforming union, freedom from the devil may indeed be our good fortune, and again it may not. God may permit his attacks and his attempts at deception, for the same reasons that he permits those temptations, which are due to our own weakness. Therefore, we can never drop our vigilance. Indeed, a tendency to do so would be an indication against the presence of strong virtues, especially that of holy prudence.

While many of the criteria usually given for the transforming union are only generally applicable, with always the possibility of a lesser grade or an outright exception, we come now to one to which there is no exception. It is not distinct from the idea of the heroic degree of the virtues; rather it is a necessary means to it. Thus we now turn to the general route of our journey.

We have already indicated that the means used in the final state of the spiritual life, are generally the same as they were before we entered it. There is sometimes a certain confusion, however, about the relative importance of two general means: the commandments and the counsels, (by which we principally mean the three evangelical counsels, those of poverty, chastity, and obedience, which our Lord gave us in the gospels). There is a tendency among spiritual people, especially some poorly informed in the religious state, to put the counsels above the commandments. After all, for example, we are commanded to receive Holy Communion once a year, and only counseled to receive every day, and obviously the second case is better than the first. Many potentially spiritual people have been disheartened by undue emphasis upon these three counsels, just as the same emphasis has had the opposite effect of blinding others, who are living the counsels, as to how things really are in the spiritual life.

Paradoxically, the truth of the matter is that the primary and essential means toward the perfection of the Christian life, are the commandments, rather than the counsels of perfection. Thus, ultimate spiritual perfection is possible to all, since all can obey the commandments, although not all can follow the counsels. The commandments concerned are principally these: "Thou shalt love the Lord thy God with thy whole heart, and with thy whole soul, and with thy whole mind, and with thy whole strength. And thou shalt love thy neighbor as thyself" (Mk 12:30-31). This command of loving God is stated without measure, that is, we are commanded to love wholly because there is no measure to the worthiness of God to be loved. Our perfection consists principally in the heroic degree of this love and that of our neighbor. All the other commandments are given to help us specifically to remove those things which are contrary to this love.

On the other hand the counsels of perfection, especially the three evangelical counsels of poverty, chastity, and obedience, are a secondary means toward perfection in that they can remove obstacles which, though not contrary to love of God, still hold us back, such as the preoccupations with making a living or the distractions arising from marriage. Although these counsels imply a more perfect following of Christ, they are not of the essence of perfection. Thus a man who is married and must work to support his family can still love God with his whole heart, mind, and strength—although his love will encounter difficulties which the vocation of another man will have largely removed.

Yet even those who are not bound by these three counsels, as are religious by their vows, must in some sense live according to the spirit of the counsels, insofar as this fits into the duties of their state in life. Thus a man should not want more of wealth than is compatible with a reasonable security. And outside of his own marriage he should be as careful of his sexual instincts as anyone who has the vow of chastity. As for obedience, he should see in all lawful superiors, ecclesiastical and otherwise, a participation in the fatherhood of God, and obey them accordingly. In these ways love of God increases, because the unavoidable impediments to love that come to all of us in life, are minimized by living the counsels.

Our calling by God will determine the degree of our use of these counsels, as well as of others such as mortification and solitude. We will always have obstacles to love of God and neighbor, no matter what our vocation. The important thing is not to love God so little, as to refuse to follow those counsels which will diminish the effects of the obstacles, as the rich young man who refused, not because of obligations to others, but because of love of his possessions. The counsels may, in an individual case, become the normal means to sanctity, even the only means which will bring close union with the Beloved. Yet the central truth is to follow Christ according to our vocation; the command to love God and neighbor is not effectively hindered by any state of life to which we are called by God, called either directly or by the circumstances in which we find ourselves here and now.

The way to closest union has many steps that must be made, some quickly and delightfully, some slowly and painfully. Not everyone who starts finishes, and so, much of hope and labor is lost if we do not finish. To arrive, to finish, we must want what we seek, and want it much. So great a gift as closest union with God is not necessarily given to those who have the natural talent for the spiritual life and all the helpful surroundings, or "else grace would no longer be grace" (Rm 11:6), but ordinarily to those who want it, plead for it, and with sincerity persevere in working out their part in it. But it can also be offered by way of a free gift, by way of exception, to anyone to whom God chooses to give it, much as he gave conversion to Magdalen and salvation to the thief on the cross. The grace of God knows no barriers.

In practice it is not enough for spiritual perfection to say that we have kept the commandments to the extent that we have avoided those things which are contrary to love of God and neighbor. We cannot be satisfied with the ordinary degree; in some ways God will ask more from those he wants to draw close, will ask what is beyond the prescribed and the merely lawful. Then his will in such matters becomes our personal law, a part of our personal vocation. Unlike the rich young man we must accept the personal call, live according to the grace that is offered, and give ourselves in love to the loving will of God for us.

Personal vocation implies guidance by God, by the Holy Spirit (to use our Biblical and theological language of appropriation). This guidance tends to increase as we advance on the way toward full union. Indeed close union with God is impossible without special guidance and help by the Holy Spirit, so prone to error and weakness is our fallen nature. Yet because of this same fallen nature, we may spoil the work even of the Holy Spirit, and also mistake what is not of the Holy Spirit for something that is. To say the least, guidance by the Holy Spirit requires that we learn his ways, and also our own tendencies toward error, especially through rationalization and an unconscious eagerness to be deluded along lines of our own weaknesses.

From such carefulness, we can see how far the perfect man or woman is from those who grasp at one or two verses of the Scriptures, forgetting all the others as well as the constant teaching of the Church, and proclaim the only law to be the inner law coming from the Holy Spirit, of whom they seem to be all but an incarnation. St. Paul indeed does tell us: "Whoever are led by the Spirit of God, they are the sons of God" (Rm 8:14), and also, "Where the Spirit of the Lord is, there is liberty" (2 Cor 3:17). But if the Holy Spirit were to be our sole guide by his inspiration alone, there would have been little reason for writing the New Testament. St. Paul himself gives evidence of the need for external directives, of guidance by and through the Church. This evidence is written in almost every line of his epistles.

Instead of proud independence because of supposed total dependence on the Holy Spirit, the person who has roots deep in the true Spirit, will find many practical applications in this life, in the words of this same Holy Spirit: "Be subject to every human institution for the sake of the Lord" (1 P 2:13). By obedience through love, we also are more disposed to the heroic degree of the virtue of justice, by which we give every man his due without regard to our feelings, or to our possible gain, or to the possibilities of evading our obligations.

Even with the saints, we are not certain that they are led by the Holy Spirit in every detail of their lives. They are not infallible in these details, as we see when Paul and Barnabas disagreed violently about the reliability of young Mark (See Ac 15:36 ff.). Both of them could not be right, and Paul is gracious enough to imply his error later (cf. 2 Tm 4:11). Similarly Peter probably rationalized himself into good faith when he ate with the Jewish Christians at Antioch and avoided the Gentile converts. But he was certainly in error, as Paul pointed out to him in forceful language (Gal 2:11).

Yet within limits, and these surely include the acceptance of guidance by the Church, the Holy Spirit now becomes the principal guide in our lives. We would expect this more and more as we grow in grace. Ordinarily, this growth enables us to reach a maturity by which we are able to make by ourselves most of the decisions in our personal spiritual life. Indeed an exaggerated dependence of total and permanent subjection of our spirit to another human being in the form of a director, seems contrary to the operation of the New Law. St. Thomas regards such subjection as an imperfection. However, imperfection must be acknowledged when it is met, and self-knowledge may uncover certain areas or circumstances in which we cannot operate without guidance.

This dependence we must accept in all humility, in all truth. We acknowledge the reasonable dependences of our lives, and do not proudly or impatiently try to live without them. Our humility is compounded both of such dependences and of the greater dependence of child to God our Father. Indeed, the particular dependences are often necessary dispositions for the essential dependence upon God, implied in the virtue of humility. As God has so arranged our nature, we will always need some helpers, and this need will arise from our imperfection and is rather always concomitant with our social, human nature. Such is also the help in the spiritual life that comes to us from the intercession of Mary and the saints and angels. The communion of Saints is God's plan from the beginning to the end of the spiritual life.

These helps and others such as the Mass, the sacraments, and the sacramentals are means toward union, none of them essentially different from those of our beginnings. Many of them have become associated with the common people. But the higher guidance by the Holy Spirit is not at all universally opposed to what appeals to the common people. These means do not change very much as we advance. Most often the change for us is to see more clearly how important they are, and to use them more fruitfully. There is hardly a more certain way to stop our spiritual progress than to reject something, which has helped us, merely because it is not "spiritual" enough, or "liturgical" enough, or is somehow associated with the common people.

What we may want to put aside in our spiritual development

can only be put aside in the clarity of knowing that it will no longer help us to get to God, and then only by asking in deep humility for his guidance rather than casting away, so to speak, our clothing and supplies in the foolish hope that the final peak is climbed by love alone, or by anything else alone. Many things have helped us, and the Holy Spirit will still use them to make us acceptable for closest union. And yet of course the principal one is love.

The promise of the Holy Spirit "to teach all things" (Jn 14:26) applies first of all to the Church. But in those areas where the individual is free to operate, we must also humbly and prayerfully look to the Spirit to guide us through others or through circumstances, and also by his own personal action. Indeed, sanctity is not possible without his guidance. No rules are adequate, and no director is wise enough to understand all the needs of each soul in the complex possibilities of life and to give the direction in which it should move. In fact, the degree of our docility to the Holy Spirit determines the degree of our spiritual development, and the degree of our union. Yet this personal guidance never has an absolute autonomy. The New Law as St. Thomas tells us, is primarily a law which is in our souls by the power of the Holy Spirit. But secondarily, and surely effectively, it is also a written law as a prerequisite for our obtaining and using the divine guidance (I, II; 106; 1).

We cannot adequately discuss being taught by the Holy Spirit without at least briefly examining the gifts of the same Holy Spirit. As to the gifts of the Holy Spirit, it matters relatively little in practice whether we know all the theological distinctions. It is sufficient to understand that we are helped in many ways by God, both indirectly and directly, and with both ordinary graces and with graces that are more than ordinary. Many saints have been made without the specific, technical knowledge of the gifts of the Holy Spirit.

If specific and great emphasis on the gifts were given earlier in the spiritual life, some spiritual persons might have unwisely sought the higher manner of knowing and acting, and have neglected the normal light of reason guided by faith. During the earlier stages, this light of reason is our normal light and the gifts provide a help from God in special circumstances. If this natural light, guided by the virtues of faith and holy prudence, were to be neglected, and at the same time the gifts were not fully or frequently operative, we would be left open to subjective and even diabolical influences. The hard and extended work of acquiring all the virtues might be set aside to wait fruitlessly for some enlightenment, or motion of the Holy Spirit.

It is only in the very last stage of the spiritual life, that the influence of the gifts of the Holy Spirit tend to become prominent, notwithstanding the probability that some of the greatest graces of our lives may have come through the gifts at the beginning of our conversion to God. Now, however, we have a man or woman deeply rooted in all the virtues, especially in humility, and habitually alerted to possible deception. Thus, it is well now to say more of the gifts specifically, when the danger of getting lost is relatively less.

There are two ordinary ways in which the human mind and will in grace, can be moved by God toward good. One is connatural in its operation. The grace of God (of God the Holy Spirit, if you will) moves us by means of the various virtues, and especially by charity, according to the rule of reason enlightened by faith. We thus do good and avoid evil, but always in the human mode of understanding and acting, with our reason at the core of it. We are also conscious that we are the ones who are doing this, even though we are also aware, by faith at least, of the help of God's grace.

The other way of being moved, is by a special movement of God, which we assign by attribution to the Holy Spirit. This differs from the accustomed movement of actual grace by the manner in which it moves us. We are moved here, not according to the human way, but according to the divine way. The quality within us which makes us docile to this movement by the Holy Spirit, is a potentiality which we acquire with sanctifying grace, and is called collectively "the gifts of the Holy Spirit."

To say that we are moved in the divine way or mode, rather than in the human way or mode, means that we are acted on in a different manner than we are by customary grace, even great graces, operating through the virtues. A good example of both ways or modes is that of a boat which can be moved by oars or a sail. With the oars the movement may be very difficult, and in any case we are aware that it is ourselves who are moving the boat. This is the human mode of the virtues. On the other hand, when we put up the sail to catch a favorable wind, the boat is then propelled in a different manner and more easily. According to our analogy, we are being moved by God in the divine mode of the gifts.

Like every example, there is something about this one that doesn't fit. With the gifts of the Holy Spirit we cannot use the sail (the gifts) whenever we want to, as we can use the oars (the virtues). Thus we can and must use the good habits or virtues to operate as needed, in our daily life. The gifts cannot be used at will. They depend solely on the will of the Holy Spirit. All we can do is to dispose ourselves for their use especially by living the virtues, such as humility, love, and trust, in an ever stronger and even heroic degree, by desiring only the will of God, and by generously submitting ourselves to it in our daily lives. Since we have these gifts from our baptism and as long as we are in the state of grace, in a sense our sail is always up, ready to accept all the help God will give us. But only when the wind blows (when the Holy Spirit acts) can the sail (the gifts) be helpful to us.

Those who have some experience with contemplative prayer, will understand this perfectly. Under the influence of the gifts, although the Holy Spirit is operating, we are not inert instruments. As with contemplative prayer, we give our consent freely to his action. Unlike most contemplative prayer, however, the operation by the gifts does not necessarily have to be accompanied by a sense of God's presence, of the divine transcendence. The gift of understanding, for instance, can give us a comprehension and penetration of divine truth without our being conscious that God is illumining our minds. In the gift of counsel likewise there may be only a deep assurance that a certain solution to our problem is the will of God. (When there is a sense of the divine in a specific *communication*, it is more likely to be an extraordinary gift, a gratuitous gift or *gratia gratis data*, which the gifts of the Holy Spirit are not.)

The gifts are distinguished from the truly extraordinary graces, such as locutions, visions, and speaking in tongues. Likewise in themselves the gifts are not "miracles of grace," as was the conversion of St. Paul. They work in close harmony with our nature, and this is the theological reason why they must be habits deep in our souls: so as to conform to God's general plan of having an instrument proportioned to his action, just as the "ear" must be perfected by the habit of a foreign language, in order to receive a direction in that language. Thus, the gifts do no violence to our nature, as if we were forced by God, but rather by them our nature is made harmonious to this movement by God.

A final defect in our example of the boat is, that the sail always remains the same, whereas the habits which are the gifts grow along with sanctifying grace and the infused virtues in the soul. We thus become more and more capable of being guided or moved by the Holy Spirit. This growth does not mean that there will come some *definite* time when the virtues will become a less dominant mode of action, and the gifts become more prominent, as when a child leaves off creeping and begins to walk. There is always the freedom of God to draw us as he will, some more in one way than in another, according to our personal vocation.

In general, however, it can be said that he will tend to operate through the gifts noticeably even before the final state of the spiritual life is reached when the gifts reach the full flower of their capabilities. This is another way of manifesting the truth that as we move onward, we reach a point where grace (the operation of the gifts, after all, is a grace from God) becomes more, and nature becomes less, that the human mode of moving toward the good is superseded by a mode that is above the human. Of course much of this human mode will be with us in our day to day living, even in the unitive way, even in our highest perfection. The Holy Spirit is not normally going to enlighten us concerning the ordinary use of our time or what to eat for dinner.

The gifts of the Holy Spirit are supernatural habits, rooted in the soul in grace, just as are the infused virtues. We usually think of habits in the sense of our being able to do something, such as the habit of walking or of writing. But there can also be habits disposing us to the action of others, such as the ability to be taught in school. Also, as with the gifts, when such a habit increases, we are able to be taught more or better, as when a student progresses in higher mathematics. Thus the gifts, like this kind of natural habit, provide a permanent basis for the Holy Spirit to move us more readily, with a facility of response that only a habit can give us.

There is never a real opposition between the action of the virtues and of the gifts, for the same God works with grace in either way for our salvation and spiritual perfection. Indeed one of the purposes of the gifts is to perfect the virtues. We can readily see, for instance, how the gifts of counsel and fortitude could strengthen the virtue of chastity under severe temptations.

The gifts are necessary for both our salvation and perfection, not because the infused virtues themselves, along with actual grace, are insufficient to bring about our perfection. Rather, the reason for the necessity of the gifts lies with ourselves. Even the infused virtues are received into fragile vessels; we are prone to rationalization, foolishness, shortsightedness, fears, and many other defects which in crucial moments in our lives can lead us away from God, even permanently, or somehow stop us at a lower level than our full potentiality.

To guide us and strengthen us consistently against defects which we sometimes cannot recognize or against dangers we do not suspect, we need the help of a higher power which works above the limited human mode and which can make us respond easily, readily, and willingly to divine grace. This the Holy Spirit does through the gifts, to develop the virtues into the heroic degree, and also to produce acts worthy of a high degree of sanctifying grace, the acts which are the fruits of the Holy Spirit and the beatitudes.

These fruits of the Holy Spirit and the beatitudes are, in their perfection, characteristics of the transforming union. The fruits indeed can also be produced by the virtues, because they denote a

certain delight in virtuous deeds. The beatitudes, however, demand that we find happiness (beatitude) in things which are so far
above human nature (poverty of spirit, meekness, and persecu-
tion, for instance) that they would seem to have to come about
principally, and in their perfection, only as the result of the gifts
under the influence of the Spirit of Love.

In considering the transforming union as a high degree of the
virtues, rather than some esoteric grace to be signaled by some
extraordinary phenomena, or even by great amounts of ordinary
contemplative prayer, we avoid much of the false ambition which
leads some to desire what is spectacular rather than what is fundamental. On the other hand, it is not false ambition to desire close
union with God and therefore also to desire the heroic degree of
the virtues which are essential to that union. Even here of course
we also risk the unconscious desire of egocentric perfection. But
in practice the commandment of love will keep us from that. A
man might really want only to see himself perfectly adorned with
all the virtues, but not if he loves. Authentic spiritual perfection
and close union cannot help but come, if we truly love God, desire
God, and persist in our best efforts to have him.

PART II

CHARACTERISTICS OF THE
TRANSFORMING UNION

Chapter 7

THE CHARACTERISTIC PROBLEM

In the transforming union we are at the summit of the spiritual life. This seems to be a simple, straightforward statement. In reality, however, the source of the confusion surrounding the transforming union is often this term "the spiritual life."

The spiritual life, in common enough usage, is taken in two meanings: one, and most importantly, the Christian life; and the other, the life of prayer. On thinking about this, we must come to the conclusion that the spiritual life is the Christian life, but that it would not really be the Christian life unless it included prayer. Furthermore, we can also say that the better we lead the Christian life, the better should be our relationship with God in prayer.

There is no one who would contradict this analysis, but when we come to the more advanced stages of the spiritual life, we find that these instead of being described in terms of the highest Christian life, have somehow become identified with certain advanced states of prayer or with certain extraordinary phenomena experienced in advanced states of prayer. It would seem, however, that this identification is illegitimate.

If we consider the spiritual life as a whole, it is no more accurate to call a man a beginner in the spiritual life (and therefore in the Christian life) just because he uses formal meditation in prayer than it is for someone to be considered in a higher spiritual (and therefore Christian) state just because he has been given contemplative prayer. Some people are drawn by God the way of contemplative prayer from the beginning and yet never bear much fruit in the imitation of Christ in the virtues. On the other hand there have been saints who have had trouble with any kind of prayer at periods in their lives when their identification with Christ would come under the general description of "perfect." Progress in prayer must always be considered as a likely step-by-step progression with the Christian life, but it is not the criterion of that life. It does not by itself tell us how completely this individual man has put on Christ nor how close he is to God in love and sanctifying grace in the depths of his soul.

The general tendency, however, is to confuse the beginners in the spiritual life with beginners in prayer. If beginners *in prayer* were simply labeled as that, some of the confusion might be eliminated. And it is ordinarily true that these would often be beginners in the spiritual life too. The real difficulty comes when it is said that a man must be given this or that kind of higher prayer in order to be considered more than a beginner in the spiritual life, regardless of the high degree of the virtues which he may have acquired by a love nourished, let us say, by constant reflection on the life of Christ, by the use of the sacraments, and by the protection and help of the Blessed Virgin.

Some of the insistence on states of prayer can be truly frightening. For instance, ecstasies and raptures are emphasized in the higher stages of the spiritual life, even when they are not insisted upon. "Raptures occur continually, and there is no way of avoiding them even in public" (*Interior Castle*, VI, 6). What father for instance, who must work to support his family, would reasonably want more than a "safe" spiritual life if he is told to expect this by following Christ more perfectly?

There can arise a great difference between the call of all men to perfection and what is described as this perfection. This is so because, instead of a map to guide us toward spiritual progress, we have largely been given descriptions of advancement in contemplative prayer, as well as visions and revelations. On the contrary there is no reason why actual grace—enormous amounts of it, but without the higher states of prayer—cannot bring about the total conformity to God's will which is the transforming union. And grace is had for the asking.

In practice this should give confidence to those who are disheartened about spiritual perfection because they have no experience of contemplative prayer (at least none that fits these descriptions) and cannot foresee any. Only grace is necessary and grace is not the same thing as contemplative prayer.

It is true that contemplative prayer itself can be called a grace just as an inspiring sermon can be called a grace. Especially in its more vivid forms such prayer can bring forth noble efforts by the love and courage it inspires. The same is true of the extraordinary gifts such as visions and personal revelations. But even so, actual grace is the essential moving force to make the increase in the virtues permanent. Only grace moves the will toward this end, and grace is in itself something unfelt. To illustrate this, using a much lower level of prayer, we have all seen people who will act with overflowing charity under the influence of emotional prayer. But when spiritual darkness comes, the charity disappears. And what was mistaken for great closeness to God turned out to have little grace with it. However, this is not to deny that vivid contemplative prayer, even on lower levels, makes the practice and the increase of the virtues easier.

On our part we are made perfect especially by love moving us toward the heroic degree of the virtues. In making a judgment, St. Teresa of Avila gives second place to all that one might experience in prayer. She tells us, "We must base our judgment on the virtues" (*Interior Castle*, VI, 8). To achieve spiritual perfection contemplative prayer is secondary to actual grace, the gifts of the Holy Spirit, the Mass, and the sacraments.

These words are by no means intended to minimize the great gifts of love in prayer that God has poured out on those who have written so well about them, as well as on others who have not written. The error is in accepting these descriptions as if they were absolute criteria of the state of Christian perfection. Indeed, when St. John of the Cross and St. Teresa of Avila are read together, one will find differences of approach and differences even as to counsel.

As to their different approach, we see in the man a somewhat single-minded captivation by the deep insights he has been granted, this to the exclusion or de-emphasis of other elements, whereas it is the woman who is here the more reasonably tolerant and more broadly human.

As to their counsels, sometimes we find them in contradiction to each other, in details it is true, but in practice important details. No doubt some of this contradiction can be intricately harmonized but the strong impression of divergence remains. Thus, they cannot be taken for the absolute authorities as often they are, in the sense that in the spiritual life things *must* happen their way. Indeed also, their divergence illustrates a basic and unforgettable principle which they both hold in common: "God leads souls by many ways" (*Interior Castle*, VI, 7) and "God leads each soul by a different way" (*Living Flame of Love* III, 59).

Paradoxically it is St. John of the Cross, one of those most insisted on as a criterion because of his inspiring descriptions, who gives us the key to understand them: that there is a diversity of ways in which we can arrive at the transforming union. He is speaking of the spiritual betrothal. In this description "is contained *the most* that God is wont to communicate to a soul at this time; but it is not to be understood that *to all* such as arrive at this state he communicates *all* that is expounded . . . nor that he does so according to one single way and degree of knowledge and feeling. For *to some souls He gives more* and *to others less*; to some after one manner and *to others after another*; though souls belonging to either category can be in this state of Spiritual Betrothal. But we set down here *the highest that is possible* because in this is comprehended all else" (*Spiritual Canticle* XIV and XV Emphasis added).

We may take as an example, St. Teresa of Avila, another admirable source of descriptions of the last stages of the spiritual life. Here indeed it may be truly said, is a soul who has received "the most" and "the highest." Yet there is no doubt that her descriptions are largely autobiographical, as can be seen from the many similarities between the more objective *Interior Castle* and her *Life*, written by herself. Thus her experience is too limited to be applied to all, too limited if for no other reason than its most eminent exaltation to "the most" and "the highest." Indeed she herself is the first to admit that there are many other ways to arrive at spiritual perfection. "He grants these favors, not because those who receive them are holier than those who do not, but in order that his greatness may be known . . . or in order that we may praise him in his creatures" (*Interior Castle*, I, 1).

Yet even St. Teresa can be brought to testify that her own great experiences which are often used as criteria of the unitive way, were not always in the high degree she may seem to indicate. Speaking of a recurring experience of spiritual "distress that I more frequently and habitually experience at present" in a life so apparently full of raptures and ecstasies, she tells us that this distress "sometimes is more severe and sometimes less so. It is of its maximum severity that I will now speak" (*Life*, ch. 20). (To speak of maximums or "the most" seems to be a characteristic of these two justly revered authors.)

Her life therefore was a much less uniform kind of life than is monolithically displayed by some codifiers of the spiritual life. Even in her life of prayer in those spiritual stages where her kind of prayer is sometimes insisted on as the norm we find that prayer had many fluctuations.

We have no way to know how much of the writing of St. John of the Cross was purely autobiographical, that is, was based on his personal experience alone, since his experience with souls was much broader than that of St. Teresa. But it seems beyond doubt that at least some of it is, not to speak of the subjective coloring that one's own experience tends to put on one's judgment. We have at least one example to give support to this. He wrote the *Living Flame of Love* after the first redaction of the *Spiritual Canticle*, and like all his works, is presented not as personal experience but as objective teaching. In the prologue of the later work he says, "Although in the stanzas (of the *Spiritual Canticle*) we spoke of the most perfect degree of perfection to which a man may attain in this life, which is transformation in God, nevertheless these stanzas (of the *Living Flame of Love*) treat of a love which is even more completed and perfected within the same state of transformation." In the relatively short time between these two compositions, we can hardly expect that a great number of people in the transforming union presented themselves to him with identical experiences. The reasonable conclusion is that these experiences were his own—to his greater glory as a saint, but leaving us with the suspicion that much of what he also wrote as objective teaching was likewise his own experience.

These reasons, as well as examples of saints whose lives were greatly different, induce us to expand into a general principle of what St. John of the Cross cautions in regard to the spiritual betrothal, that "the most" and "the highest" is also the content of the descriptions of the spiritual marriage, that is of the transforming union, and that there are other people in this same union who have had less, perhaps far less of the spiritual favors described by the mystical authors.

In the process of going from primary sources to those who summarize the thought of the primary sources, "the most" and "the highest" have somehow become the norms by which all are to be measured once they set their eyes on spiritual perfection. Thus, people will become discouraged, and others may give up their own way as planned by God, and begin to watch for the things described. This last is surely a way not to find God very deeply, because our attention and our heart must be on him and not on phenomena. This results in a blindness which may even prevent us from seeing, or appreciating the experience of love that God may actually give us in a muted or hidden form—to say nothing about our thoughtlessness in regard to his greater gifts, such as the redemption, his friendship through grace, and his constant but unnoticed protection. In looking for "the most" and "the highest" we may never really have understood what was actually happening.

This limitation on the works of the great mystics by the fact that they speak of "the most" and "the highest," is one of the basic ideas we must take into the later spiritual life. If we never forget it, we will avoid many deceptions of the devil and of our own imagination, and will be in less danger of losing the path which God has planned for each of us.

In higher contemplative prayer there sometimes have occurred two spiritual events which should be noted here. One is spiritual betrothal and the other is spiritual marriage. In a book which attempts to clarify spiritual perfection we will not attempt to list, or to evaluate the characteristics often given to distinguish the one from the other. Even St. John of the Cross experienced difficulty in describing them. In the short time between the first and the second redaction of the *Spiritual Canticle* he transfers from one category to the other 14 out of the 29 stanzas concerned, almost half, together with the bulk of their explanation—and not all authorities seem to agree with the changes. Our purpose here is only to look at them for what they represent, two sharply defined stages of spiritual development. In doing so, we will assume and not repeat the same criticism already made of the spiritual marriage alone, and of course still caution against any implied universality of mystical characteristics, as we have just finished doing.

In speaking of the transforming union we have been speaking principally of what is called the spiritual marriage. Thus, the meaning of this term has become somewhat familiar. Spiritual betrothal cannot be said to be greatly different from this; many of the characteristics listed are very similar. What is principally lacking is the same quality that is lacking in human betrothal in respect to marriage: permanence, especially in the presence of the Beloved, and the closer union. This in short is what spiritual betrothal is said to be.

In favor of this terminology it must be said that the relationship is a logical one; before complete union there is obviously a period of very close, but not yet complete perfection, allowing also for degrees within the union itself. The unsuitableness of the relationship, however, can be shown by two facts. One of these has been mentioned before, that the betrothal has been an actual visionary experience of some of the holy women. In conformity with this, others have attempted to substitute other mystical experiences which are not visionary, but rather are a certain vivid variety of contemplative prayer. Indeed one wonders in passing if the very force of these two metaphors themselves, both of which imply intimacy of varying degrees, is not a reason for some of the insistence on the great intimacy of contemplative prayer in the higher stages of the spiritual life. Enough has been said for the present about his alleged necessity, however.

The other fact in opposition to the relationship implied by these terms is that the spiritual life is normally a growth, that is, a gradual process. Thus, as an example, it would be very difficult to know exactly the day on which a boy became a physically mature man. He grows to maturity gradually. But betrothal and marriage do not happen that way. Betrothal indicates a determination and a promise. It happens on a definite day and hour. Even more so does marriage, when the whole pattern of life immediately changes. Thus there arises an arbitrary need of an explicit spiritual event in every case in order to support the terminology, and for which event there is even less evidence than for the great amounts of contemplative prayer allegedly required.

In dealing practically with people who aspire to close union with God, a director will find that this terminology can sometimes be the source of much useless concern. He is questioned whether this or that experience of fervor could be the betrothal, instead of the great concern being about ways to show God greater love in one's life, and to avoid falling away from the level already reached. With this terminology it is greatly more difficult to see the one train going on the same track throughout the spiritual journey.

Like the descriptions of spiritual marriage, those of the betrothal are also full of "the most" and "the highest," and this is a disadvantage in practice, as we have indicated. But on the other hand, if we consider the term "betrothal" as meaning love given and love received, together with a determination to give all in complete union—surely included in the idea of betrothal—then the term would seem to apply too broadly to be of much practical use.

The best way to grow in the later spiritual life is to want God just because he is God, to want him very much because he alone is worthy of our full giving, and to want him because we love him. Then just as in life, in the slow process of growing, the time comes when we are in our full maturity, so in the spiritual life we can find ourselves in the full possession of God, and of what gives us the objective assurance that we do fully possess him namely, the heroic degree of the virtues. And contrary to the descriptions of the mystics, but true to life, we may not be able to tell the exact day it happened.

The great mystics are God's masterpieces in what he is willing to do with those he loves, even while on earth. Thus they are a witness that God can show our fallen humanity almost unbelievable manifestations of his love, but they have a further usefulness for us. Through their experiences we can become aware of some things that may happen in the transforming union, and not consider it deception if the same or similar experiences should happen to us or to someone under our guidance.

Moreover, even when they cannot be our guides, they can still be an encouragement. Even when it becomes most probable that we are not being led in this way, we can still see in their experiences a small amount of what will be ours in an eminently greater degree in the next life if we have the sanctifying grace and supernatural love to merit it.

Besides the characteristics imposed on the perfection of the spiritual life by too great an insistence on contemplative prayer, there are lists of other characteristics based mainly on the ascetical life or on certain virtues, such as humility. These may or may not be useful in individual cases. Some of them demand so little that anyone who is seriously overcoming his faults would seem to be in the unitive way. Others are so restrictive that they would make the gate narrower than our Lord said it was. Thus they are not the gospel nor are they likely to be our personal way of reflecting the gospel.

Instead of being a repetition or "the most" and "the highest," this is a book about "the less." That is, it is a book which gives the basic requirements of the great closeness to God which is called the transforming union. No individual can be certain that he will get "the most" and "the highest" of what are broadly called the consolations of God in prayer. He must be prepared to achieve perfection solely with what God has planned for him. Our lives are always the fulfilling of our personal vocation, the freely designed plan of the ever free God.

Within the general way for all men or for all true followers of Christ, each life is a personal way by which each one must go to God. This, as we have said, becomes a personal law. To miss this, because we look for something objectively better, is to risk missing our own potentiality to sanctity. If, as it is truly said, the better can be the enemy of the good, then sometimes the best can be an enemy also.

The concept of personal vocation respects the freedom of God in the matters of the amount of contemplative prayer a man or woman will have in the transforming union or in their whole spiritual life, for that matter. There have been faulty opinions on this, as when many held that mystical prayer was for the chosen few, such as those with a special mission. Humanity was thus segregated with the far greater part automatically barred from such "extraordinary" prayer, as contemplative prayer was held to be.

On the other hand, there are others who hold for a moral necessity for infused contemplation in order to arrive at spiritual perfection. But if we look closely at what they mean by moral necessity here, it is that *in the majority of cases* sanctity will not be attained without it. This of course is an admission that there is a minority of cases in which sanctity will be attained by prayer below this level.

The truth is that there are not two classes of people in this regard but many individuals. We cannot speak with certainty about majority and minority; obviously we cannot make an adequate census of souls to find out. Nor can we predict the way even individually for anyone. We do not know the hidden plan of God for each soul. But speaking, as we must, tentatively and professing only probability, we can say that all of us who are seeking God can look forward to the possibility of some contemplative experience of God at some time in our lives.

This belief is based, not on reasoning, but on trust that God who loves will not fail to show himself, even perhaps dimly, at some time to every man and woman who is seriously seeking him—not to speak of the many whom he will call to seek him by initiating such a personal experience by way of invitation. Each of us will receive the amount and kind of contemplative prayer that God portions out for us individually, be it a single experience or a habitual companionship. When it happens it is always a part of the ordinary way for each.

Likewise it is also true that, although contemplative prayer is in the ordinary way, this does not necessarily mean that all who persevere in the attainment of spiritual perfection will be led to a constant or frequent overwhelming experience of God. No one knows whether he will be called to this or not. Thus the personal vocation solves a problem in practice which great scholars may debate endlessly in theory. No matter what is said, the individual must wait for God who is always the initiator of each act of infused prayer. Therefore, from our spiritual beginnings to any point along the way we proceed by disengaging ourselves from any alleged universal necessity for such prayer, especially in great amounts, and go to God by whatever prayer helps us—especially by the prayer of petition for the graces to lead a life of great virtues in following Christ.

Thus the theoretical question, as to whether great and frequent mystical prayer is a characteristic of the transforming union, seems to be answered too. Even if we freely grant that this kind of prayer may happen in many of the lives of those in this state, the fact that some can still attain the same perfection without it, indicates that it is not of the essence of the transforming union, and cannot be a necessary characteristic or property. It is incontestable that essence and properties must apply to all in the group.

In practice our personal vocation principally concerns the means toward the fullness of our degree of loving God, although indeed vocation is always a higher and broader concept than the means. The individual will not ordinarily reach his full potentiality of loving God, unless he finds and uses the means (including the kind of prayer) which God has portioned out for him.

Even though a given set of means is a part of our personal vocation, God is not limited in the omnipotence of his action. In that sense of his omnipotence, he can bring about the greatest and deepest love through any given set of acceptable means, as for instance, he has made saints in both the married state and the religious life. In the set of means he has chosen for us we can come to love him intensely for himself alone, no matter whether we are drawn by the highest contemplative prayer or by something very much less. God's grace is always the effective cause of our perfection, and it knows no obstacles among the various means at his disposal.

Although in general the means of our sanctification remain a personal necessity throughout our lives, it can happen that a particular means may have to be diminished or discarded. Or it may be used on a higher level, with more insight, or with greater purity of intention. In the perfect detachment required of perfect love we must be prepared to relinquish any former means when it becomes clear, or at least highly probable, that God's grace is no longer in it to draw us closer to himself.

To arrive at certainty, we are helped by prayer and the courage to find out by trial and error. We watch closely how God is acting with us when we seek him: Does he give us grace without this means, or do we find ourselves still reaching him with it? Or is the particular means found to be unnecessary or even burdensome to the spirit? Or does the spiritual life without the means become boresome so as to be precarious, boresome because we are trying to proceed without the grace provided by the means? We must trust the Holy Spirit for these answers. Since there is a definite way for us, he is bound by his own nature to make it clear for us, in his own time. Suddenly to throw away any hitherto helpful means, because we have read how someone else has been led by God would be to waste what he has given us.

The purpose of means is a more positive element in our spiritual life than detachment, but the general principle of following our individual way is common to both. In general the attitude toward change is the same for both at this point in the spiritual life. Even though more positive action can be attempted in regard to the means, in these latter stages we must in general let God make the changes in our life rather than to trouble ourselves about seeking new paths.

Chapter 8

"NOW MY EXERCISE
IS LOVING ALONE"

Writers have become accustomed to accept certain experiences as the norms or essential elements of the final stages of sanctity. As a result we can overly desire that what we read be true of ourselves and thus miss the really essential elements by looking for these frequently mentioned, but non-essential phenomena.

Even when we have become convinced that love is the principal practical element in the transforming union, we are still apt to confuse love with a state of prayer. Instead of love being conceived essentially and sufficiently as a oneness of will with God and an overflow into our lives, we rather expect to be able to love God continuously in vivid awareness, to be constantly absorbed in him so as to know nothing else, or better, to have him in a loving intensity and still be able to fulfill our duties at the same time. The general impression is that the transforming union is a continual state of contemplative prayer, of uninterrupted, intimate communion with God. This of course is the way God may act if he so chooses.

It will be helpful to examine whether this general impression is the actual experience of those who have written about it. The evidence from the two greatest mystical writers is otherwise. St. John of the Cross is very specific. He is commenting on the verse, "When I went forth. . . . That is to say, this favor has completely passed away; for although the soul be forever in this high state of marriage . . . yet it is not forever in actual union according to (its) faculties. . . . The faculties are . . . very frequently in union . . . the understanding by knowledge, the will by love, etc. . . . The union of the faculties is not continuous in this life, neither can be so" (*Spiritual Canticle*, XXVI, 11).

St. Teresa of Avila is even more revealing. "You must not take it that the effects which I have described (in the Seventh or highest Mansion) . . . are invariably present all the time. . . . Sometimes our Lord leaves such souls to their own nature, and when that happens, all the poisonous things in the environs and mansions of this castle seem to come together to avenge themselves on them. . . . It is true that this lasts only for a short time—for a single day, or a little longer at the most" (*Interior Castle*, VII, 4).

These are only two of the great number of those who in the history of the Church have had God as their companion at the end of their lives. But since these two are sometimes alleged in favor of continual and intense intimacy, we may wonder if other cases not recorded so candidly, are not similarly exaggerations of the facts. Perhaps what happens is the same as when a person writes cheerful and interesting letters home. Those reading them would form an impression greatly different from the truth, that it is as a life without heartache or monotony. Thus the biographers of holy people may unintentionally give a one-sided impression, having perhaps only a few scattered facts or having to compress many years into a few chapters.

Both in the lives of some of the canonized saints and in authentically reported accounts of other people who will probably not be selected for canonization, some more or less habitual state of God's presence seems to be an established fact. We should and do rejoice that some of us have been chosen by God to end our lives as if the door of heaven were partly opened. Our principal objection, however, concerns the tendency to make this very desirable familiarity an essential characteristic of the state of the perfect. We submit, first of all that this is not so, and secondly that it is harmful for it to be considered so.

Over against the admittedly marvellous favors which God has given to some of the saints, there is one striking case which puts an end to all dogmatic insistence that the spiritual life must terminate in such favors. There is a principle in all *a posteriori* investigation, (scientific investigation is a good example) that we cannot make true universal statements which apply to all possibilities. In science we say that, although it takes numerous experiments to establish a law, it takes only one contrary experiment to disprove the law. And so, against all the beautiful pictures which show us how a saint is supposed to end his life on earth, we have one (at least) well-documented, contrary experience, that of St. Thérèse of Lisieux. By her own person she disestablishes any demand that a soul in the highest degrees of grace be as the classical descriptions say it must. She really reestablishes in fact, that here as everywhere else, God is free.

Her case is admittedly an extreme one. Although she surely had periods of contemplative prayer during her life, and on one occasion so strong that she thought she would die if it were prolonged, her life ended in the darkness of pure faith. We do not have to try to investigate the cause of this darkness; this would be useless because we have in hand a greater truth: it happened. Under the all-embracing providence of God, this chosen soul was not presented with raptures, ecstasies, or a consciousness of God so intimate that the world of the present and the world of the future seemed almost merged into one. Instead, this God, who always knows what he is doing, gave her darkness.

With this the point has been proven; the easy universals of the spiritual manuals have been broken. No one of us can expect that God has reserved the ecstatic states (any beyond) for him. No one of us can suspect that he is not entirely close to God because it hasn't happened to him. And perhaps as a result of this more of us will get to the closest union with God, because we will look more to the essentials and less to the description of states which God may never give.

If God permits sanctity to exist along with the total darkness of much difficulty in believing, hoping, and loving, then there is no reason why in other souls he cannot bring about perfect sanctity by trials of lesser intensity. If he chose in the case of St. Thérèse to have the light totally obliterated, in other souls and in different ways he may allow light only intermittently. If this were understood, these souls could move toward God with the same assurance as she did, where now they lack the spirit to press on confidently to the goal because they don't fit the descriptions.

While it is true that an exception to a law can break the universality of the law, here we may be said to invoke this principle too strongly. It will perhaps be said that, generally speaking, all the perfect ended their lives this way, and that those who did not are exceptions. And since there are always exceptions, these exceptions only prove the rule. God, it will be said, almost always gives himself fully and constantly to perfect souls, and the few exceptions are made only because of special circumstances.

This does not seem to be true; it would mean that God has made too many exceptions. We have the example of the many saints who to the end of their lives were almost wholly given to apostolic and charitable work, as were St. Vincent de Paul and St. Francis Xavier. We do not deny even in busy men the general existence of contemplative prayer in a high degree. But does the evidence support the generalization of a constant living in vivid awareness of the two worlds, or even almost exclusive awareness of the next? Are there not, as in every life, periods of ordinary light as well as great light, and even times of storm and darkness? A sober reading of the lives of those saints whose interior life is written by themselves, and not second hand, will indicate that even for the perfect, life has undulations.

We have already seen that both St. Teresa and St. John of the Cross, agree with this. But St. John of the Cross sings so happily,

> "Now I guard no flock
> Nor have I now other office,
> For now my exercise is loving alone"
> 						(*Spiritual Canticle*, XXVIII).

But was it? Certainly not in the sense that he did no work. In the later part of his life, after he had written these words, he successfully holds high offices in the reformed Carmelite Order, founds several houses of the Order, is deprived of his office by intrigue, and dies an unwanted and mistreated guest in a house of the very Order he helped to found, or reform, if you wish the word. His sole occupation was surely not love in the sense which many people take and which more than one soul, who has not read the saint's own explanation, spends useless time hoping for, and perhaps trying vainly to bring about.

One of the most vivid self-portraits of a saint is one which is almost neglected by those who attempt to draw the portraits of the typical saint. This is the man, St. Paul, as portrayed in his epistles and in a lesser degree by St. Luke's account of him in the Acts of the Apostles. Here we have a man who is perhaps more like Christ than any other. Here is also a man who at one time even had a glimpse of heaven. Now this man, who was also confirmed in grace, has given us a look into his heart in the many epistles that span his life as an apostle. We look in vain for the serene, unperturbed, solely heaven contemplating saint. Instead we see a man who intensely loves God and Christ, but who suffers physically, mentally, and spiritually, who must carry the burden of the Church, the burden of a body never far from death, the accusations and plots of his own people, and the inconstancy and sins of the Gentile converts whom he was enriching with Christ. If God treated St. Paul this way, he can treat us this way. And if we are treated this way, it doesn't mean that we haven't arrived at more than moderate perfection and must still look to some artificially contrived ideal for our life's pattern. It may well mean that we too, having "fought the good fight and finished the course," are also looking forward to "a crown of justice," and yet find ourselves living very much in this world, even as did this great saint.

Our Lord's innermost life is complicated for us by his having the beatific vision. But the external pattern of his life, for example the suffering of the loss of Lazarus, his weeping over Jerusalem, and his agony of soul in the Garden and on the cross—all at the end of his life—all give no assurance that an absolute retirement to do naught but love is the expected pattern of our lives. We may even suspect that this accepted pattern is the exception which has somehow slipped into the books as the rule.

Even if we were to consider an exception, the total darkness of the last months in the life of St. Thérèse of Lisieux, her life still is of practical value in our discussion. Since God has made her life so different from the stylized lives of the saints, we must admit his freedom. What he did for her in great degree, he may do for anyone in less degree. We cannot therefore *expect* that God will give us the constant joy of his close presence at the end of our spiritual life. We cannot build our life on such an expectation. Instead we build it on something better, the solid and even heroic degree of the virtues, especially trust in him and an all-pervading love of him and of neighbor.

This kind of love, which is not always a pouring into the soul, or a pouring out of the soul in great and delightful torrents, is what St. John of the Cross means by saying that love is the sole occupation of the soul. The soul sees everything as love of God; its conversation with God, which is a second nature to it, is more concerned with love than anything else. It lives love. But many times it is an ordinary, hardly felt kind of love. Sometimes it is even a forced kind of love. Only when God wants the dull earth of the soul to become transformed, does the fire blaze up to heaven enkindled by the fire that has come down.

When we say that the whole occupation of the advanced spiritual man is to love, we therefore must be careful not to understand that he now does nothing but love. Rather we must understand that he now does everything out of love and sees God's love, in everything. He is also moved much more by true love for neighbor. Love becomes the atmosphere he breathes in and breathes out. Thus, he is said to love God continuously.

In this increasing oneness of our will with God's, and in the love that underlies it, we can say that our love for God is constant. Even when we are distracted by our duties or by recreation or by sleep, we know that God is unchangeable, and that his love is always there. When our minds are free, we enter into it. Love becomes our whole life; we live only for the one we love and for his desires in this world. But instead of the loving intimacy we were told to expect, there may simply be a union far deeper than anything we can be conscious of without special revelation, a very close but unfelt union in sanctifying grace.

Transforming union can have no deeper meaning than that of sanctifying grace, by which we become in some way sharers in the nature of God. If we love him, this oneness, unseen and unfelt, will be our treasure and joy, accepted in faith and held onto in hope. We will be content to wait for the actual revelation of this oneness when we will see clearly, face to face, what he is, he of whom we are sharers.

Any conscious awareness of himself and his closeness that he may give here can be the beginning of that eternal reward. However, it is always more of a means than a reward, both to strengthen or comfort us on the way and to cause a thirst for more of God, to make us want even more the completeness of union in heaven. Thus, what we see and experience of God on earth is always less than what is unseen and unfelt, that is, always less than the union through sanctifying grace.

Chapter 9

LOVE IN THE HEROIC DEGREE

Despite the relative inability for the descriptions of higher contemplative prayer to lead us into the transforming union, a judicious reading of the primary sources, such as the *Spiritual Canticle* and the *Living Flame of Love*, can very forcibly lead us to the essential means for entering this union. Not surprisingly, we find that the teaching is the same as in the Scriptures: the first essential means is love. This should not surprise us, of course, but it may be disappointing. The descriptions have offered us exalted states of prayer, not to speak of truly extraordinary, and yet it is simply love, both as the first and the second great commandments, love of God and of neighbor.

Anyone who would almost separate sanctity from what is possible to ordinary mortals, and who stresses mere phenomena, fails to see the essential oneness of the spiritual life. Here is the golden thread that runs from beginning to very end. Love is what makes the beginner rise from sin, makes the proficient acquire the strong habits called virtues, brings him through the Dark Night (if God so wills this for him), draws him into a new relationship with the light within him, and can (again, if God so wills) carry him out of himself into God in the ecstatic states and beyond.

So it is love of God and not any expectancy of some state of prayer, which we must accept as the essential means of closest union with the Divine Lover. Our life must be more and more love, love spoken to God over and over, love lived with God in the language of the heart without speech, love that becomes the breath of our whole life—but not necessarily at any given moment a differently felt love than that experienced along the way. It may be a love we almost have to force out between our teeth, or a love that is a desperate cry in the darkness. Be it this or the love that seems almost one with the light, our life becomes essentially an act of love.

Love is the bond of the transforming union, making one burning torch out of all the other elements. Of all the virtues that bring about this union it is the most important. Since we cannot seek it in what may not be given, in great emotional transports or in vivid contemplative rapture, we must seek its perfection elsewhere. We must seek it in some concept which implies the highest degree of it and yet does not require nonessentials. We find this in the command of our Lord to love with the whole heart, the whole soul, the whole mind, and the whole strength.

This first and greatest of the commandments has been known and accepted by us from the beginning of our spiritual life. Perhaps for this reason we unconsciously look for something better at the summit. The answer to this, however, lies in the word "whole." It is true that this commandment can be observed in a greatly imperfect manner, in the bare avoidance of mortal sin, in that a man does not break the union of love as such sin implies. But just as there is a minimum fulfillment of the law of love, there is also a perfect fulfillment.

We do not have to be told that our progress toward the total giving of ourselves is usually a gradual process. Our previous spiritual life stands in evidence. But we may have to be reminded that progress by steps is still the norm in the final stages. Even in the transforming union there are degrees of transformation. For instance, we receive an insight of grace or are placed on a certain level of conscious oneness of mind and heart with God. Then strangely and disappointingly, all seemingly becomes ordinary again, but the grace and the level of oneness are not lost by disappearing. Their work is done deep in the soul. And although we may not see the essential transformation there, God sees it. If we are faithful, the effect becomes always deeper and more pervading, and the union always closer.

From our own experience we can learn a lesson. Since ours is a normal human experience, it can be applied to other normal human situations. Thus, if the story of our lives were written in terms of these clear but inconstant insights and infrequent intense oneness, those who read them would think that our lives were made up of little but lights and consuming fire. Once we settle on the fact that the mystics were men too, and that they felt and operated much as we do ourselves, we may be able to read their words, not (let us hope) losing their inspiration, but surely with a deeper understanding of what their lives actually were like.

The totality of love by which we love God with our whole mind and heart does not necessarily have to be a spontaneous pouring of our whole being into his. For some indeed it has been this; for all some of this probably has occured at times during these later stages, but again not necessarily in a great torrent of emotion or a flight of the spirit. Perhaps rather it was a silent oneness, little more than momentary, in which the soul embraced the will of God completely and to the depths of its being. However, at times other than these, the love of the whole mind and heart may have to be something willed throughout the ordinariness of each day.

The wholeness of our love makes of ourselves a wholly pleasing offering to God. The rebellions that still exist because of the false primacy of the self, are now no longer willed. Even the first movements of our fallen nature, those small, involuntary divergencies which happen before the will can become alerted to them, these are steadily decreasing because of the increasing oneness of our will with God through grace.

Even our formerly unruly instincts are now harnessed into bringing us to God. For instance, the natural tendency in many of us to seek the highest may have been a powerful force for selfish ambition. But now it becomes a part of the new person, which impels us to seek the truly highest: objectively, God, and subjectively, our closest union with him. The whole heart is brought to God, in such a case, by the whole mind being given to him.

There will be many personal ways of entering and growing into the transforming union, as many as there are ways in the spiritual life itself. Each man must find his own way, the way God is drawing him, or he will not arrive. But basic to all these must be the total, habitual choice of God and his will, and this in a high degree of intensity.

From one point of view sanctity is a total conformity to the will of God. We must love the whole will of God with our whole will. God's will can be considered in two ways: his positive will, by which he actively or actually wills something pleasing or distasteful to us, and his permissive will by which he permits some good or evil to happen. Both aspects of his will must be loved entirely and intensely.

The positive will of God is ordinarily no great problem for someone who has come a great way in the spiritual life. That we must love God in the good things he sends us is so obvious and easy as to need no comment. Neither are there any great difficulties about the positive will of God in matters of direct punishment. God's love is proven when he punishes, and we can love that love even if it is hard to do so. The same is even more generally true of suffering sent directly by God, not as punishment, but as, for example, reparation for others or for the good of the Church. This sort of suffering, however, would often seem not so much directly willed by God as permitted.

There is more difficulty with the permissive will of God. For one thing, God does not seem to us to be so directly involved in this as he is in his positive will. For instance, if we are not being directly punished, then there isn't the direct relationship with him which makes suffering easier to accept. We have now come to love him so much that loving him is far more important than anything he could do to us. Besides this, however, the issues involved in his permissive will are often much more enormous.

There is the matter of permitting good things to those who do not deserve them, and this is the complaint of many of the psalms. It can almost be called the scandal of God: the suffering good man perceiving notably wicked, unjust, or godless men prospering and to all appearances quite happy or at least living pleasantly and comfortably. There are many reasons which we can offer to excuse God for his apparent aberrations, but in the end there must be trust in this wisdom and in his ultimate justice or his mercy.

Above all we must love his will which can seem so contradictory to the simple justice which we instinctively demand.

When God permits evil to happen to good men, the problem is even greater, because this kind of evil is the hardest fact to reconcile with a loving and all-powerful God. When the innocent must suffer disaster or misfortune in which they are not personally to blame, when God permits failure to attend the most dedicated efforts of good men for good causes, and allows the triumph of evil, we will find it easier to be distressed by the evil than to see God's part in it. We question, rebel, fear, or lose heart, when in simple truth we must love. Even if the majority of Catholics should apostatize, except for a small handful, we must love the will which permits it.

This does not mean that the evils will not hurt. They may even break our hearts. But it does mean that we can draw closer to God by loving this difficult will, instead of becoming insensible to him under the appalling tragedy. We understand that God is one in nature, that his permissive will is actually no different from his whole nature, not therefore different from his love. This can bring us peace in the greatest personal and general evils.

Not every love can be called heroic love. Heroic virtue implies some great ability to endure the difficulties of life, whether they be difficulties which anyone would call enormous, or whether they be difficulties enormous only to ourselves because of our disposition or condition, not to forget the enormous difficulty of daily fidelity in little things. Heroic love is seen in such endurance, and it began in our purification from the self-seeking, both blatant and subtle, which is at the heart of what separates us from God. Also, when we say "Thy will be done," we need to know what this will is. The agonies of soul sometimes experienced in finding that will, and wanting only that will, despite the tortures of uncertainty, this too can be heroic love. By more than one such dark road do we arrive at perfect love.

We must want God's will as carefully as if we were slaves and he solely a severe and exacting master who would punish us for every conscious deficiency. That we now desire to do all for love should not make us any less careful and assiduous than if we worked only out of fear.

Yet without love we will not arrive at perfect love. Heroic endurance of difficulties was known even among the pagans. To bring about this union with God, our endurance and action must have love for the principal motive, not always explicitly, but a love always more completely permeating our will.

It is the will which is the most important here. Heroic love must never be confused with great emotion. Emotion by itself is not virtue. Yet, all the emotions are the creation of God and when under control, are not to be despised in the spiritual life. They can fortify the will to accomplish difficult deeds and thus help us to increase the strength of the virtues.

Nor must heroic love be confused with great transports of love as sometimes occurs in higher contemplative prayer. St. Teresa of Avila tells us, "You must not build upon foundations of prayer and contemplation alone, for unless you strive after the virtues and practice them, you will never grow to be more than dwarfs" (*Interior Castle*, VII, 4). Generally, however, such love, as it is described by the great mystics, will indicate the heroic degree of the virtues. Yet it is usually looked upon by them as a help rather than a proof of anything. "These favors are given to us to strengthen us in our weakness . . . so that we may be able to imitate him in his great suffering . . . His Majesty can do nothing greater than grant us a life which is an imitation of that lived by his Beloved Son" (ib.). But rapturous love, though surely very helpful, is not necessary. God's grace is able to accomplish all that God wills.

Any kind of experience of love must still be proved by our works. When we say that "the measure of loving God is to love him without measure," that measure must certainly fill all the small places of our lives. Even though the loving desires felt while in prayer may reach to the skies and fill the earth to its ends, their fulfillment is what proves them. Heroic desires have their place, even when some of them are unfulfillable, for love wants to do all for the Beloved. The test of heroic virtue, however, does not concern laudable but impossible desires. Rather, the test may be waiting for us at our fingertips, things like the love of God in great suffering or reverses, or love of neighbor in forgiveness of great injury.

Love in the heroic degree does not necessarily mean love in a vivid degree or love enjoyed over an extended period of time. At the very heart of heroic love is the conformity of our will with God's, not only the desire to be conformed, but conformed in all things, a quiet intensity which is the result of wanting it out of love. We must not become frightened by the word "heroic." It is love that is asked and not heroic works or heroic penances, and this should encourage us. But even more, heroic love comes not so much from ourselves as by the grace of God, and to this high degree of love God would lead us all as we would lead a child.

Chapter 10

DESIRE FOR GOD

Love of God can be such a simple, delicately marvelous experience that it is usually better not to question it. We can come to much confusion, for instance, by wondering if our love is sufficiently unselfish for what we expect love to be in the higher reaches of the human spirit. But the truth is that our love is basically no different here than it has been all along. Even now it is not completely unselfish, nor will it be even in heaven. Even there we will still love God because it is a delight to love him, and here we will *enjoy him* also, as St. Thomas is so fond of saying (E.g. II, II; 24; 9. See also *Spiritual Canticle*, XXXVI, 1, 2, 4).

Enjoyment is a secondary quality of our love. In our more mature spiritual life we love most of all with the love of friendship, the love that loves God for what he is and seeks his good rather than our own. We wish to turn even our delight to his glory. Unlike our love for human beings we must, both by nature and grace, love him more than ourselves. And thus we desire that he be glorified by our love more than that we should be delighted by it. But we must not think of this distinction at all times.

Just as human love is increased by the desire for the love, the voice, and the presence of the other, and can be increased by mutual companionship, so our love for God is increased by our longing for his presence and by our delight in this presence when it is given to us. Quite truly we submit to his will when this is not given, but our wanting it surely pleases him, even as it would a human friend. And since it pleases and glorifies him, the love of the desire adds to the higher love we give him as friend which seeks first the good, that is, the will or the glory of the Beloved.

While not being essentially different from our previous love for God, our love now has become gradually purified. It becomes like the growing in one kind of love while diminishing in the other without, however, entirely losing it. Our love of God at first is apt to be somewhat self-centered, similar to the earlier human loves of our life. We look to God for help, for defense and protection, and we want much of his consolation. As we make progress, we learn to live without these consolations, but we still look upon God as somebody to fulfill *our* plans and *our* will, rather than the opposite.

The more perfect love, that of friendship, by which we love the other for himself and principally wish his good, is often a late stage, which of course has many degrees. In the spiritual life we come to rejoice, for instance, in our Lord's resurrection because it gives us hope, and also because it means his triumph and his present happiness, just as we would rejoice in any good thing which comes to our friends. We await his Second Coming for such reasons also. We come to love God more because of his goodness and because of what he is. His gifts and protection, even though they are more in evidence now, become a secondary consideration. When we receive an obvious favor from him, the fact that it is he who gives it, becomes more important than the favor itself.

Rather than to say that there is a conflict between the virtue of hope (by which we trust to receive something from God) and the highest love of friendship (by which we love him exclusive of his gifts to us), we can instead see a higher kind of hope. Besides the love that is friendship, we can also hope to give God a love which pleases him by the very fact that this love of him delights us beyond measure, and that he is desirable for that reason along with the other and better reasons for loving him. This love of desire is the praise that our being gives to him for what he is *to us*, and we delight that this increases his glory, even if only a little and even though not essentially.

We have been emphasizing here the goodness of a love for God which is our good. The reason for this is that we must again encounter the problem of language. Some of the mystics speak as if they had found a love that seeks no reward. We are, of course, now on delicate ground. Yet if we do not want to risk the unreality of quietism, we must search for broader understanding than is given by the immediate words of these mystics.

The mystic is not rejecting happiness; rather he is prescinding from it here and now. What he has and wants more of, is God. This absorption into God, and the resulting oneness with his will, causes him to cry out with only part of his mind, that he is indifferent to all reward. But on the contrary he, more than any other, *wants* this God who is carrying him out of himself. The full possession of God and the possession of happiness are really inseparable for him. The important point for him is that here and now God is not making him happy by the gift of something created but by the gift of himself.

St. John of the Cross has many words against the desire which many have in the beginning of their spiritual life, the desire for the emotional consolations of prayer. But we read him imperfectly if we attempt to apply this to the whole experience of God in the life of prayer, especially toward the end. "Now that the perfect union of love is made between the soul and God, the soul desires to employ and exercise herself in the properties which pertain to love . . . praying for three things which are proper to love. First, she *desires to receive the joy and sweetness of love*, and for this she prays him. . . . The second desire is that she may become like to the Beloved, and for this she prays him. . . . And the third desire is to delve into the things and secrets of the Beloved, and to know them, and for this she prays him" (*Spiritual Canticle*, XXVI, 3). Since the spiritual life is the beginning of the life of heaven, we should not resist, indeed we should welcome and prudently desire some of the joy of God's presence in this life, if it be his will.

The authentic voice of God in the Scriptures is not squeamish about reward. Our Lord openly commands in the Sermon on the Mount: "Store up the treasures for yourselves in heaven. . . . For where your treasure is, there will your heart be also" (Mt 6:20, 21). This treasure of course is capable of various meanings, and surely God has various treasures awaiting us as St. Paul indicates (1 Cor 2:9). The great lovers of God know by an experience which transcends cold faith, that this treasure is overwhelmingly God himself. In an ultimate sense both our highest hope for reward and our purest love are found in this one marvellous being, and without contradiction. Our ultimate self-interest and our highest love, both are the possession of God, in a love so absorbing that it neither seeks nor cares for anything but God himself and his will here and hereafter.

So great is this desire for God that St. Thomas (II, II; 24:9) and St. Augustine (In prim. canon. Joan., Tract, v) tell us that the desire for death because of love is a sign of perfection or of the unitive way. In saying this they quote St. Paul: "I long to be freed from this life and to be with Christ, for that is the far better thing." As a characteristic of perfection it must also include the full meaning of St. Paul, the willingness to forego the reward here and now because of God's will, "Yet it is now urgent that I stay alive for your sakes," the urgent need of the early Church (Ph 1:23, 24).

This double sign, both the great desire for death out of love, and the willingness to remain on earth for the good of others, indicates the great strength of the two kinds of love, that of desire and that of friendship, in the perfect person. Sometimes this state of soul is called holy indifference to life or death. The use of the word "indifference," however, seems to miss the great tension that is involved. We would hardly call the above words of St. Paul an example of even holy *indifference*. Sometimes in trying to raise us to the heights, our language can dehumanize us.

St. Teresa's desires for death were sometimes close to causing it. No one can read of the enormous "distress" she describes (*Life*, ch. 20) and not see in it the same tension of which St. Paul writes in fewer words. Yet her desire is not acquired by reason nor by disillusionment with life "for it is certainly entirely supernatural and comes from his hand." Nor does it come from pure faith or love, for it is an accompaniment of a certain kind of contemplative prayer which brings pain, "the ways of the cross," and at the same time "comprises a delight of exceeding worth" (ib.).

Since it was a grace coming from contemplative prayer, this vehement longing for death may not justly be called a characteristic of the unitive way for those who do not have much contemplative prayer. Their acceptance of life or death therefore will be a more moderate experience also. An indication of how St. Teresa adjusted herself to these desires can be inferred from the fact that she lived about twenty years more, most of it in great activity, after she wrote her *Life* at the command of her confessor.

Nor can the desires for death which pour from St. John of the Cross be described as complete indifference either. "The soul addresses this flame, which is the Holy Spirit, with great yearning, begging him now to break this its mortal life in that sweet encounter, so that of a truth he may communicate to it perfectly what it believes him about to give to it whenever he meets it namely, complete and perfect glory" (*Living Flame of Love*, I, I). "The soul makes answer: 'Perfect me now if it is Thy will.' Herein she makes the Spouse those two petitions which he taught us in the Gospel, namely: 'Thy kingdom come. Thy will be done.' And thus it is as though she were to say: Give me this kingdom perfectly if it be Thy will—that is, according to Thy will. And that this may come to pass: Break the web of this sweet encounter. . . . The soul speaks here and calls the encounter 'sweet,' for it is the sweeter and the more delectable inasmuch as the soul believes it to be about to break the web of life" (ib., 28). Indeed St. John of the Cross repeats this desire so often in his works on the last stages of the spiritual life that one wonders how the so-called "indifference" has come to be listed as a characteristic of the transforming union.

Thus it can be said that the perfect man does not have to express insistently a willingness to live. Although he is wholly dedicated to the will of God, he may desire death rather than life, because his insight into the mind of God brings him an assurance that God too wants his death soon. If this were not so, the holy desire of some of the martyrs would be contrary to the state of perfection, as with St. Ignatius of Antioch who prayed that the lions would not refuse to kill him as sometimes they did refuse to kill other martyrs. Such an insight into God's mind may come to a man reasonably because death is a logical solution here and now to the pattern of his life, or because his death would involve a charity to those who must care for him. Obviously there is no reason to hold back desire for eternal union when the medical situation promises release shortly. Then submission to the will of God finds itself in the patience to allow God as many days, weeks, or months of waiting as he wants, as did St. Thérèse of Lisieux.

Merely looking forward to death is not a necessary sign of the unitive way. It should always be present in those who are this much in love with God, but obviously there are other people who desire death for other reasons and yet, may think it is principally for love of God. Such reasons may be the loss of loved ones, any of the disappointments of our true or false hopes, the loss of possessions, including health and integrity of the body, or it may even come from a melancholic disposition. Of course any of these causes can be present along with a true desire for death as the doorway to eternal union with Eternal Love. Indeed they can be a disposition for it in the sense of removing the natural obstacles to this desire, for death is by nature a horrible disruption of the union of soul and body. We shrink from it with an instinct that has no ordinary exceptions, so great is our grasp on the familiar, on life, and on the body.

As we approach the union with God which preceeds the final union with him in the next world, the body becomes less important than previously. In many of the earlier stages of the spiritual life, the body presented problems on the one hand, and on the other it became a loved companion or a means of finding one's identity along with the other self-knowledge. But now as we draw nearer to the eternal embrace, the natural love for the body can be a means of holding the soul back. For one thing, existence with the body is the only kind of existence the soul has known. There is the natural fear of the unknown. There is also dislike to think of this beloved companion suffering the corruption of the grave. It is even hard, psychologically speaking, not to indentify oneself with that corruption.

In the natural process of aging, much of this preparation for the disruption of body and soul takes place naturally and gradually. The body becomes more and more of a burden and one becomes more willing to cast it off. God's providence is surely seen here.

But what about those who are called to God while still in the height of their powers? Some more voluntary means may be necessary in order to bring about the same result as a natural willingness to leave this world. The best way is concentration on God; in his love we forget all else, and are willing to sell all for this pearl of great price. Indeed in the love of God somewhat less attention will be given to the body as a consequence.

There are also direct ways of not giving the body so much attention. This does not mean a real neglect of one's health or of one's cleanliness or appearance. But in small ways less can be done. Indeed God will do much of this for us. By gentleness rather than by neglect or brutal treatment we will best prepare to shed this beloved body as we would an outer garment, in order to enjoy the embrace of God's love in its fullness. It may also help if we gently remind the body that it too has an eternal destiny of beauty and delight after the resurrection, which will seem to come shortly once we are with God.

We can also be held from desiring to be with God in eternity by our love of life in regard to the good, beautiful, and attractive things of nature and of the world. It is not that our hearts are now being held from him as such, but rather that we are held to this life when God would begin to prepare us to leave it. It is one thing to have a definite obstacle between the soul and God here and now, and quite another to have as a general obstacle this beloved and familiar earth, the beloved people and the beautiful things of earth, which we must leave in order to have God and another, unexperienced life in heaven.

In the first instance, of being held back from God by a definite obstacle, we eliminate the occasions as far as we can, and we meet those we cannot eliminate fortified by the strength from the Mass, sacraments, much prayer, and self-discipline. These things can be used or enjoyed only with the purity of intention by which we do what we are doing principally because it is God's will, even more *because* it is God's will than any natural attractiveness they may have. But in the second instance, we seek rather a lessening of the hold we have on life itself.

Our obstacle is human nature itself in one of its deepest

instincts. We want God, but instinctively want earth also. We may not be as prepared as we ought when God comes, nor so greatly desirous of his coming. This is clearly the case of some old people who cling desperately to a life which they ought to be eager to cast off.

The practical solution to the problem requires more than ordinary discernment. Few of us will have a revelation of God's design in regard to the moment of our death. One hesitates to advise following the instincts of love, because more than once in the lives of good persons love has outrun the designs of God. Souls who thought themselves being prepared to come to God found themselves remaining on earth for long periods of time instead.

Despite the fact that we ought to be prepared to die at any moment, is there still not a difference in the way we must live over the long period and the intensity with which we can bring to the short time of immediate preparation, if such is given to us? If life is to end, as we ought to desire it to end, in a maximum of love and desire, could we then not eliminate much which would be needed if we were to live a much longer time? But on the other hand, if we must live for many more years, we must be careful not to lose what may be needed for the fulfillment of our duties. Nature and the good world are so designed as to bring us happiness of their own, and such pleasure can be used, and can even be necessary for our union with God.

Furthermore, besides what could conceivably be eliminated in preparation for the eternal vision of God, there are other things which cannot voluntarily and ultimately be given up. Our obligations may well continue to be present along with a sense of urgency in regard to the next world. The duties of our state in life can require that nature and the world continue to be used despite their hold on us. Married people, for instance, will use the beautiful instincts of their bodies in their love. Many occupations require involvement with the enthusiasms and concentrations which come with material things. None of this, it would seem, should be eliminated or changed just because a strong pull is felt.

Perhaps it is better to leave things in the hands of God. In putting aside only what clearly interferes with union here and now, we are acting in harmony with a plan which will bring us infallibly to our final preparation if we follow it.

But surely in some rare cases, the instinct or even the certainty for more immediate preparation will be present. Relying strongly on the virtue of holy prudence, we can in practical ways cut some of the threads that bind us to earth and could keep us from the God we love so much that only his will prevents us from running into his arms. This is not a forcible separation from the enjoyment of everything of earth but a gentle and peaceful reorganization of our lives when we see that this separation is prudently advisable and will not upset our spiritual progress by pulling our roots that are still sources of life.

This desire for union with God through early or immediate death can be spiritually dangerous. It can be a source of illusion in relation to some possible communication from God, and can be psychologically enervating. In this way it can unfit us for doing God's will on this earth and result in the neglect of duties and of practical love of our neighbor who must still live in the conditions of this world. However, each of us has an appointed amount of work to do and an appointed time to stop working. None of us can do all the work we see to be done. If we are close to God, he can make us see this clearly. Perhaps then it will be his merciful will to call us home.

It is the opinion of great saints like St. John of the Cross (*Living Flame of Love*, I, 30) and St. Francis de Sales (*Treaties on the Love of God*, VII, 11) that some of the souls close to God will die of love, actually die of love at the moment, of death, regardless to what clinical causes may be present to cause death at any given moment. St. Thérèse of Lisieux died with the words, "My God, I love thee," as have others whose names will not be recorded. May he give to those of us who have sought him consistently, through success and failure, through our failings and great need for his mercy, this way of falling into his eternal embrace.

Chapter 11

ALONE WITH GOD

The desire for God carries mortal men through enormous difficulties of flesh and spirit. Yet they consider that they have done nothing when these are compared to the possession of God, to the friendship (no matter how dim it may seem at times) of him who is life and love. The holding to such a desire is no small gift of grace but it would not be possible if he did not also draw us and push us past the enticements and rationalizations which would cause us to stop wanting more and more of him. At many points we could have stopped and been content, thinking that this was all there was to be had of him, so pleasant was it to have this much of him and so many other things besides.

For this reason God counsels man and at times also intervenes in his life so that man will "remove from himself whatever may hinder his affections from attending wholly to God, for it is in this that the perfection of charity consists" (II, II; 186:7). Loving God with the whole heart means that we must ever deny the self and take up the cross. Under grace love increases by many means, one of which is by detachment. And if love is to increase, detachment must in some sense increase also.

It is a truth both of theology and experience that the working of grace becomes more evident to the soul in the latter stages of the spiritual life than in the earlier. Both in prayer and in action we learn to depend more on the action of grace than on the exercise of our own powers. The same general dependence upon grace is also true in the matter of detachment.

In the earlier stages of the spiritual life, God may let us see his beauty and goodness through his creation, especially his human creation. Later on, without entirely withdrawing this way of finding him, he wants us to know him more directly and intuitively. We would expect this of love. But we who have loved creatures in ways that partially shut out the Creator are not apt to understand this at first. A struggle ensues in which God is patient but insistent. In the end we will see how much love of creatures, including love for ourselves, was in our attraction for the Creator. But God would be less than a true lover if he did not want to be loved for himself, for what he is in himself.

In the earlier stages of the spiritual life the soul is like a block of rough marble out of which a statue is to be carved. The first task, that of chopping off the large pieces is obvious, both as to the fact that it must be done, and to the relative facility with which it can be accomplished. Here is the major work of the disciplines of the ascetical life. These can safely be imposed even by a novice in spiritual direction, provided of course that they be modified to fit the individual.

But these disciplinary rules and exercises eventually become second nature so as no longer to advance the soul greatly toward God. They have no urgent power to increase the wholeness of mind and heart for God. It is then that the problem of further detachment or purification becomes acute. The soul may still have to go through purification very deep and very severe. The problem has become one, not of removing large chunks of marble to form a general outline of the statue, but now of shaping the marble into sinews, muscles, and the features of the face.

It is precisely here where spiritual directors are most apt to fail. They may continue to work with the large chisel and mallet which were so successful earlier. Their vision is colored by what they themselves have experienced (and this is often less than that of the penitent) or by directives they have read out of handbooks of spiritual theology, directives that are necessarily general and incomplete. The wise director will watch and observe more than he will prescribe. He will make his work very little more than one of reassuring. He can do this both by his perspective of being outside the soul which is immersed in the process of being despoiled or is emerging into new life, and by his adequate knowledge of sound theological principles.

The answer then is to allow God to act more. He is the infinitely capable craftsman and his is the ultimate artistic vision. He knows infallibly both what the soul is to become and how to bring it about. This is what theologians mean when they say that we are led more by the Holy Spirit, by the gifts of the Holy Spirit, in the later stages of the spiritual life than we were at first. So now we do best by allowing him his way in the despoiling process rather than by rushing at the task as soon as we suspect a chance glimmer of light. Since the soul is being tried deeply, beyond what it ever thought it would, perhaps in the long Dark Night, we can cause spiritual harm, as well as lasting psychological damage, by trying too hard and too ineptly to purify ourselves.

In practice this means to allow God to have his way. Without excluding all possibility of our own action, in general it is better to allow God to act for us in our final purification. His action will either directly affect the object of any hidden attachment, or will clearly affect our mind in regard to it. He is more anxious for our perfection and advancement than we are ourselves. He knows what to do, and he will not fail to do it. We will begin to see our life, even our external life, changed perhaps slowly, not always without struggle and a feeling of uncertainty, but still accurately and adequately.

It would seem that when one is to enter the later part of the unitive way, the externals of his life should gradually undergo a great change. One would expect that he would give up everything except the grimly necessary so as to become more wholly absorbed in the spiritual. Undoubtedly there is some truth in this. We will find moments for prayer where they were not before; we will make certain decisions as to the relative value of things in order to be with God more often and to belong to him more perfectly.

Yet in these decisions a great care must be exercised. The soul is not yet in heaven where it will have the light of glory in order to give it the strength to live in the full light of God's presence without exhaustion. Here, though the presence is perhaps sometimes very intense, we are not yet so strengthened. In order to keep balanced and to keep God, we may find it best, by and large, to live the kind of external life to which we are accustomed. The story of St. Aloysius who said he would remain at recreation even if he had only a very short time to live, is not just an example of fidelity to God's will in the present moment. It is also great wisdom when it is stretched out across the broader picture of the months and years.

So we will most probably continue to take what interest is good in the affairs of our surroundings, will still enjoy some of the beauty of the world, must still take adequate recreation, and in general will not be very much externally different from what we were before God drew us into this final state.

Many changes will take place in the soul itself, it is true, especially in the greater desire for God and the awareness of the greater need for purification. Here in the awareness of this need we may attack the statue with an ax in the hope of helping. But instead we may break patterns of thinking and acting which are our personal way to God, some of which must be retained much longer, and others surely forever. We want to stand alone, victorious in our accomplishment, to have an angel made of light emerge from the marble. But we are always bound, by being human, to the definite order of human perfection, to its general means of commandments, Mass, sacraments, authority of the Church, and duties of our state in life, and to our own particular manner and needs in achieving it.

While it is true that we will generally continue the outline of the life which has brought us to this state, still under the influence of grace there is undoubtedly further purification from imperfect attitudes and subtly harmful attachments. What we could not see before, or perhaps would not, we now see and judge. The final and even the smallest surrenders are made. God ever becomes more the totality of our lives. We now in reality, and not only in desire or in general intention, live entirely for God, whether by faith or with some degree of his presence.

More than one man or woman has been frightened by the spiritual life, because it has been apparently divorced from love, which principally gives it meaning and some of the strength to overcome. This fright has sometimes come from the use of a term loosely and carelessly applied, the *nada* (nothing) of St. John of the Cross. When we understand the *nada*, not as a disembowelling death, but as a companion, often gentle, always firm, of our journey toward love, we will accept it as we must, as the loving instrument of the loving God.

The *nada* is not to be applied as the total elimination of all love, all desires, or all pleasure except what is directly associated with God. Nor is it a detachment so total that we no longer permit ourselves any feelings or emotions. It does give us, however, a simple word which we can use to compare what is of God or for God with what is not. Nothing or no one must have power to draw our attention away from him voluntarily, needlessly, and from within when we are at prayer, or to draw our wills from him in our life outside of prayer. Therefore the *nada* serves to identify easily what should be our attitude toward persons and things when they intrude into the aloneness of our communion with God or into the will's oneness in seeking him first.

In reading St. John of the Cross, one must understand the passionate nature of this great lover of God. His mind is so fixed on the attainment of God, that he uses language in an absolute sense which must be taken in the context of his whole purpose. Thus, as an example, he says much against desires in his various writings, seemingly as if no desire could be allowed. And yet, especially in his later writings, such as the *Spiritual Canticle*, he is full of desires for God and the things of God as we have just noted in the previous chapter. Therefore we conclude that his underlying meaning in condemning desires is directed only to those desires which do not in some way lead to God.

It would seem wisest that we interpret him similarly in the matter of the use, pleasure, and love of created things, and sometimes he gives us the indication to do this. He speaks of "attacks upon the reason made by sensuality with regard to some *disorderly* act," (*Spiritual Canticle*, XVIII, 8. Emphasis added). If our sensuality were not disorderly, it should not be considered an attack;

indeed it might lead us to God, indirectly as in helpful recreation, or directly as when moving us to God by the grandeur of the sea or the mountains.

The urgings of this great master are concerned primarily with the states of prayer which, in his experience, are a part of the higher states of the spiritual life. Generally, while in this prayer it is very essential that the soul not be turned from the intuitive enjoyment of God's presence to the things of the senses and reason. The direct attention to either of these will destroy the close oneness which the soul is experiencing with God. Therefore, in his zeal he cries out against the senses and all else which will impede this prayer.

In general God is more likely to come to us in the union of contemplative prayer when we are detached from created things, but this detachment does not mean total obliteration of everything created. It implies only that God's creation not draw us from God. For if it does, then our prayer as well as our whole spiritual life, will be that much more difficult because of it. In the end we must be able to give ourselves wholly to God in prayer without any other real concern at the moment, other than the engrossing oneness with the Beloved. Thus, for instance, we can have friends who are deeply loved, but the thought of them will not have the power to hold us back from prayer because they are loved in God. This detachment in prayer, however, does not usually come without its corresponding detachment outside of prayer. Perfect love must mean perfect detachment, which is not always a negation of use or love, but always a practical affirmation of the proper order and value of persons and things.

This order and value is taught us by God himself. We are to love God with our whole heart, our whole soul, and with all our mind (See Dt 6:5 and Mt 22:37). Everything outside of God must somehow fit into that "whole" and that "all" with which we must love him. To the extent that something of ourselves or from ourselves is given to another, or anything is taken for ourselves, and at the same time takes away even minimally from that "whole" or "all" to be given to God, to that extent we must firmly say "nada."

The *nada*, therefore, does not mean an absolute nothing but God. Even the extreme case of the *nada* of Christ on the cross had room for the consolation of seeing the fidelity of his mother and his friends. But not all of our life is intended to be that extreme, just as not all of Christ's life was that extreme either. We who seek God even in the full sense in which all else is nothing in comparison, will find ourselves more firmly in possession of those things he wants us to have. "Seek first the kingdom of God and his justice and all these things will be given to you besides" (Mt 6:34).

The *nada* applies to persons and things we love, but not in the sense of total elimination. They are still ours but not in the sense that we possess them of ourselves. We give them to God and remain content with *nada* but him. He in turn gives some of them back to us. We regard them as gifts but not as gifts totally possessed. Rather they are gifts still depending on the will of the giver. Usually we will find that we love these persons and things more deeply and richly, but they are still God's and we enjoy them only to the extent of his will, but for some of them it may be his will that he take them.

Detachment basically means that we offer all things to God in willingness of mind, that he may take them if he wishes. Likewise it has been true throughout that we know the value of what we give, and know it clearly and even agonizingly; we always come to the difference between being willing to give all and the actual giving. But with increasing clearness the *nada* becomes a companion to our life, gentle but uncompromising—or if God can get our love in no other way, then rending and uncompromising. In either case it is an immeasurably great gift, because only in the wholeness of our giving comes the wholeness of receiving from God. But the *nada* does not always come by merely reaching out for it. Sometimes, still as an undeserved grace, it comes only by much pleading.

We must not make a life of total suffering an ideal. The spiritual life, even at the highest, does not mean all possible self-denial, not all possible crosses. We must, if we would have God, follow Christ. But our Lord spent many years in the company of Mary and Joseph, surely not without great happiness. His public life too had moments of tranquil happiness with his apostles and friends such as Lazarus, Mary and Martha. But what God wants of us he must get; what is needed for increasing love we must give.

Close union with God, however, is not brought about by merely eliminating what is incompatible with the degree of union to which we are being called at the moment. As in every human love our lives will be fulfilled only if there is the companionship of love. Thus arises the question of solitude for God. The spiritual person needs and desires it as the way to God himself. St. Thomas is clearly on their side. In contrasting the two kinds of religious life, the eremitical and the communal, he says that the latter is preferred for those who are being schooled in perfection, whereas solitude is fitting for those who are perfect (II,II; 188:8). His reason for this is that God is our final end and, in a basic sense, our all. We are made for him indescribably more than for any other. To be able to give ourselves to him in the degree implied by intensive solitude is the perfect response to this basic aspect of creation. Thus we may be never less alone when alone.

There are some cautions, and St. Thomas gives one in the context. If a person undertakes the solitary life without being practiced in perfection, he risks "very great danger." Often enough he will not know whether he is this perfect. He may easily interpret as a positive desire for great solitude what is really a neurotic withdrawal from associations he finds difficult to bear. But a neurotic has no place in complete solitude. He needs the contact with others to keep him in balance, and he needs the distraction of physical reality to keep him from the unhealthy fears, illusions, and moods to which he is subject.

A more basic objection to complete solitude, however, is our vocation. God has designed each of us for a definite vocation, and although we may feel greatly drawn to certain aspects of another vocation, it would be impossible or greatly difficult for us to live that vocation as a whole. We have before the words of St. Paul: "Let each remain in the vocation in which he was called" (1 Cor 7:20). There are of course exceptions to this principle, but even a healthy desire for solitude should not have us packing a few belongings to go to the desert or to some eremitical religious order. There are always the needs of our neighbor. When these needs are a part of our vocation, we may not give them up even out of the love for God in solitude.

God can provide many ways for extended solitude if he desires it for us. A change of residence, the death of those close to us, our necessary confinements, our inevitable old age all provide ordinary ways in which God can manifest his will. These can be considered a call to quite a complete solitude if we find ourselves strong enough to endure the separations that it demands, separations from much that is ordinarily needed and dear to human nature. Such solitude, though offered by God, often is still left up to our own choice. It can be filled with distractions or not. Some of these we will probably need, at least at times in the form of recreation and human companionship. The way to find out is by some trial of solitude in varying degrees, seeing if we are closer to God, or more at peace as we are withdrawn from the contact with others and with things which seem to be unnecessary. Until God gives us an extended opportunity for solitude, we must use well the portions he gives us, this of course without harm to ourselves or neglect of our neighbor by too complete a withdrawal.

The progress of the soul toward God means leaving behind many things which would prove to be impediments. But there comes a time when there is little more to leave behind. The spiritual man has been so purified that there is little or no attachment to material possessions, to the health of the body, or to things of ambition. What love he has for persons is a love that is shared in God. God is the end, the underlying purpose of all his friendships.

Yet there still is a way in which further purification can take place. The soul has learned to love solitude but now what is asked is aloneness. This is not the same as loneliness, although actual loneliness is at times a part of this detachment, but loneliness is a negative thing. Aloneness is a positive thing. It is a certain aloneness with God.

One might be surprised that this is listed as an advanced purification, for must not the soul have been alone with God, at least in prayer, much of the time? Surely to reach even a reasonably high degree of purification, we must have spent much time alone with God in love and in searching of ourselves, seeking for obstacles to our love. But really have we been alone? Perhaps some men have. But others surely will find that they have hitherto gone to God with others, and necessarily so. They were not strong enough to go alone and needed help and companionship on the way. Those who have given advice, example, encouragement— these are the helpers and companions without whom the soul would have not made what great progress it has, and these are loved with a relatively pure love.

These others have given a support which was needed to face God. In our insecure state we might not have had the courage to face God, or to bear the difficulties of the spiritual life, for that matter, if it were not for others with whom we feel a oneness. The courage we lack to face God in the blinding light of higher contemplative prayer we can get because we are helped by this oneness with others, so that we have now a strength borrowed, as it were, from the group or at least from someone else. Besides being able thus to face God, we may also be able to accept intimate love from God because of others. Other loves make us feel acceptable by association, and by the fact that we know others are praying for us. Unconsciously, we may not believe in ourselves enough to accept the fact that God loves us intensely for what we are.

When we are thus (often unconsciously) supported by these others there is a certain lack in love which God would remedy. God chooses that we love him as he deserves to be loved, just because He is Who He is. He also wills that we see that he loves us, not because of the support of the others, but just because of what we, this person, are to him.

This is indeed the consummation of love. We are now alone with the Beloved. All others at these moments of approach to God recede into the background. They are not loved less—indeed they are loved more and better. They are not loved for what we thought they were. Blinded by our need, we formerly could not see nor allow ourselves to see imperfections in them. Now they are loved with a higher love that sees the greater truth of goodness through the truth of the imperfections. God is trusted too. The heart knows that the loved ones will receive better from the hand of God because we can now love in aloneness, than if we were to spend much time in prayer for these others individually. Yet we will often pray fervently for others and for the Church, but under the movement of grace.

In this aloneness a man goes about daily duties, daily obligations; he keeps appointments, he meets friends. Outwardly little is changed, and what is changed is done either by God's providence or by God's evident will expressed by a sure inner instinct supported by reason. Other than that, we do not urge or hasten the process of actual spoliation. We see that in God's providence we must still help others by normal human ways. We accept the inner aloneness, accept the periodic loneliness that may come with it, but we do not try to cut off all others. This aloneness requires a far more delicate touch than we can bring to bear. So this actual detachment, if there is to be any, again is largely left in the hands of God.

We see clearly now that we belong to God in a way we can belong to no other—words which we said many times before, but like many words they now reveal a deeper meaning. What external help we still need is taken in moderation and peace. We will have helpers; we will have friends. But we will have no companions, none at least who will be companions of the soul. God himself will be our companion and to an increasing degree, our guide.

We must not be surprised at a possible loss of spiritual companionship, or at least of certain aspects of spiritual companionship, which we may previously have enjoyed. It is quite true that in one sense there will most probably always be companionship of mutual love and respect. However, there is less and less outpouring of the intimate spiritual longings and experiences to the other, just as there comes a time when there is less need to be understood, encouraged, and even instructed. That part of the relationship generally has been transcended. We now love our friends even more deeply than ever, and appreciate even more what the other is. But we do not exchange so much.

5

A false attitude on detachment from created things can also impel people to stop asking God for things. In the later stages of the spiritual life we ordinarily desire fewer things and with less intensity. It is true also that prayer does grow into the overwhelming desire for God's will to be done, the most merciful will that he can bring to the situation. Many things about which we were once concerned can now be left to his love and providence by our acknowledging our need and poverty in general rather than in the particular. But carried to an extreme, as if we were exempt from the common duty of asking him for things in particular, this would seem to be a false spirituality. Instead of the spiritual child who is not above the simple act of asking, we would probably find a deformed soul, made a dwarf by spiritual pride.

A reason for the ordinary development away from the former great emphasis on asking is the greater preoccupation with love. Love has fewer needs and, on the other hand, it has greater confidence in the mind and heart of the Beloved. There is also a commendable awareness that we do not always know what God's will is and so cannot ask for some particular favor with any degree of certainty and therefore of intensity. But there are certain things about which there is no uncertainty: for instance, our need for great amounts of actual grace in order to come yet closer to God, our need to be more and more purified for his greater love, the great need of protection from our own weaknesses, and of course, such things as the good of the Church, of individuals, and of the whole world. So even though God reads our love and answers many of the petitions that are there implicitly, the prayer of petition is a duty from which we are never entirely exempt.

In fact in a certain sense our duty can be even greater because: "When God is loved, he responds to the petitions of his lover with great readiness" (*Spiritual Canticle*, I, 13). So at times we will find ourselves moved toward the prayer of asking, and this movement should not be neglected in favor of some unchristian sort of detachment. The Scriptures do not tell the perfect to stop asking; the command is for all. And we find perfect people like St. Paul doing it, not to speak of Christ praying, as he did for Peter (Lk 22:32). Perhaps one of the greatest reasons that many people do not love God more is that they rarely and poorly ask for the grace to do so.

In summary, detachment from whatever would deter us from God is as necessary as the more positive desire for the will of God. Indeed, looked at it in this way, it is a positive thing because it has a positive goal. Because of the way that absolute expressions become distorted and affect people adversely, we really ought not to speak of total detachment even in the perfect, unless we qualify it with some such phrase as total detachment by eliminating all that is in the way of our perfect union with God. What we love and what we must use of this world we do with purity of intention—unless or until we come to see that even with the purest of intentions this person, situation, or thing is keeping us from God.

For there are certain of these which will not lead us toward God, no matter how much we would wish it. This happens either because the created good is incompatible with further progress, or because God does not give his grace for its profitable use. In such a case our wishes and consequent rationalizations stand against him. But unless, or until we see this with reasonable clearness, we continue to use it with the knowledge that God wants us to use it, and we use it out of love since it helps to bring us to him. None of this will affect the union with God which requires essential aloneness with him.

So we delight to be alone with God, delight to love. We feel no pressure to discontinue love in favor of something practical, unless this be a duty or true charity. We are content, as all true love is, just to love and to be with the Beloved alone.

Chapter 12

GOD IS NOT ALONE

In our love for God we find that he is not alone. The first great commandment does not obliterate the second, no matter how much God is loved. Rather it absorbs it into one whole. No one sees better than the perfect man or woman the truth of the theological principle that love of God and neighbor are not two virtues but one.

The difference between theology and practice is often very great. There are those who would have everybody work for their neighbor almost as if there were no first great commandment, keeping God's portion to the bare minimum when even that is not made impossible. Against these, the words of Christ stand in unchangeable opposition; the command concerned is "the greatest and the first" (Mt 22:38) and this must be shown in practice or we will have God's violated honor to judge us.

When we consider the last stages of the spiritual life, the emphasis is likely to shift the other way. The principle is well stated by St. John of the Cross; "There is no better or more necessary work than love. . . . For so long as the soul has not reached this estate of union of love, it must practice love both in the active life and in the contemplative; but when it reaches that estate it befits it not to be occupied in other outward acts and exercises which might keep it back, however little, from that abiding in love with God, although they may greatly conduce to the service of God; for a very little of this pure love is more precious in the sight of God and the soul, and of greater profit to the Church even though the soul may appear to be doing nothing, than all these works together. . . . Therefore, if any souls should have aught of this degree of solitary love, great wrong would be done to it, and to the Church, if, even but for a brief space, one should endeavor to busy it in active or outward affairs, of however great moment" (*Spiritual Canticle*, XXIX, 1-3).

This is true in principle, but in practice can the perfect man now urge this against his superior if he is a religious or a priest, or if he is not, against his clear obligations to family or to other elements of his personal vocation? Because it was not the way chosen by him who is the Way for us, he should at least hesitate. In this chapter we shall endeavor to explore this problem but first of all let us note that the statement of St. John of the Cross is not as absolute as it seems.

In speaking of the spiritual marriage he says, "Let us rejoice, Beloved. That is to say, in the communication of the sweetness of love, not only in that which we already have in the habitual joining together and union of both, but in that which overflows in the exercise of effective and actual love, whether interiorly with the will in an act of affection, or *exteriorly, in the performance of works belonging to the service of the Beloved*" (ib. XXXVI, 4. Emphasis added).

Neither he nor St. Teresa of Avila were able to practice the solitude he suggests, during great portions of the years they were in the transforminig union. In fact, she is even more emphatic on the subject of love of neighbor: "The surest sign that we are keeping these two commandments is, I think, that we should really be loving our neighbor; for we cannot be sure if we are loving God, although we may have good reasons for believing we are, but we can know quite well if we are loving our neighbor. And be certain that the further advanced you find you are in this, the greater the love you will have for God; for so dearly does His Majesty love us that he will reward our love for our neighbor by increasing the love which we bear to himself, and that in a thousand ways; this I cannot doubt" (*Interior Castle*, V, 3).

Since love of neighbor is enjoined upon all of us as Christians, it becomes even more our duty as perfect Christians. How then are the perfect to love their neighbor? Our Lord's familiar answer, "as yourself," is a quotation from the Old Testament (Lev 19:18). What he himself did was to settle forever the controversy over who is our neighbor, by the parable of the Good Samaritan. All men are our neighbors and all men are to be loved as we love ourselves. This would seem to be enough work for a lifetime, but our Lord asks of us something more.

In his last words to the apostles spoken on the night of his agony, our Lord gave us a new insight into love of neighbor. "I give you a new commandment: love one another; *just as I have loved you*, you also must love one another" (Jn 13:34). This gives an added dimension, proposes an added perfection to our love, even more than that of the second great commandment. In the words of St. Thérèse, "He not only required us to love our neighbor as ourselves, but would have us love as he does." The perfection of this new commandment is in the model it offers us. Too small now is even the enormous love we naturally have for ourselves. Now the perfect model for our love is the supernatural, godlike love that Christ has for us. When we see that he loved the worst of us enough to die for us, when in particular we see how he loved Peter who would deny him and Judas who would betray him, and also see the way he has loved even us in our denials and betrayals, we can understand what this new kind of love means.

We are so accustomed to using the perfect men and women of the New Testament as examples to inspire the imperfect that we forget that, since these saints are perfect people, they become more and more an example for us as we approach perfection. Our Lady for instance, loved her neighbor with insight and generosity. When she heard of the pregnancy of Elizabeth, she knew she would be needed and hastened to go to her. She could have said, "I'm going to have my own baby. I have no time." But she didn't. Again at Cana she could have made the obvious comment, "*They* got themselves into this. Let *them* worry about it." But again she didn't. Perhaps this is one reason that in the gospels Christ did not directly make spiritual marriage a personal relationship with each individual soul, so that we not forget the truth that a man is never exclusively alone, but always with the other members of his Mystical Body. Principally it is this whole conglomeration of people, the Church, which is the bride of Christ.

The spiritual life must build certain walls between the soul and the world. Those will vary according as each man is called by God. But the walls are not without windows and doors. The spiritual life is not intended to end in a cruel unreality which seeks only love of God and nothing else. On the contrary the great commandments of love are to be observed in a manner that, humanly speaking, can be called perfect. This perfect manner of loving applies not only to love of God, but also and obviously to love of neighbor. "If we love one another, God dwells in us and his love is fully developed in us" (1 Jn 4:12).

We expect to find great love of neighbor in the saints and of course we are not disappointed: St. Stephen praying for those who are stoning him; St. Paul willing even the impossible, to be separated somehow from the Christ he loves, provided that the Jews who are now thirsting to kill him will be converted. How much better for our own spiritual life if the transforming union were normally described in terms of great love of both God and neighbor rather than in states of mystical prayer. We unblinkingly accept this heroic love of neighbor in the saints as belonging to them, but the truth is not always so strongly impressed that it is also an essential condition for our own perfect union with God.

There is a species of contemplative prayer which should be mentioned here instead of later under the forms of contemplative prayer. It is the contemplative experience of the fact that Christ is in his brethren. This, of course, does not have to be an experience which is infused, as it must be in order to be truly contemplative in the sense in which we are using the word here. It can also be the projection of deep and sincere faith aided by the imagination, an experience which can be called contemplative in a broad sense and, no matter what it is called, is certainly an insight to be treasured. As a contemplative experience, however, it comes from God in a direct manner, with the clarity and authority that the soul may have found in some of its contemplative prayer already.

The reason for mentioning it here is that often the presence of

Christ in his brethren has come to mean the totality of religious experience for people whose particular interest is in action for the needs of others. Their tendency is to put the whole of religion at the service of man, even though they may not deny God's rights for the love, worship, and service due to him who is supreme and completely transcendent to all creation. This last is never denied by Catholics, if they know that Christianity means always putting God and the rights of God first, but in practice it is sometimes neglected by a determined and almost exclusive emphasis elsewhere. Yet wisdom and experience, as well as Catholic teaching, tell us that we must love our neighbor for God's sake, not God for our neighbor's sake.

At this stage of spiritual perfection, however, it is hardly necessary to speak of excess of attention to the needs of our neighbor. Those who have come this far will not have come without a high degree of the virtue of holy prudence. This together with the gift of counsel will enable them to know what is the norm, what is the will of God for their activity in the particular circumstances of their lives. All this flows from their personal vocation, something they probably have also grasped clearly by now.

For the same reasons there is no need to speak of excess in the affective loving of our neighbor. We can now love others more deeply than previously, even more than when we were in danger of being carried away from God by an excess of what we then considered great spiritual love. Now we are more aware that our friends belong to God much more than they belong to us. Also, we want them so much for God that we would rather have separation than have either soul held back from God ever so slightly. Our former rationalizations tend to disappear the more our desire for God gives us the courage to see all things in their truth.

Not only have the lessons, perhaps hard lessons, been learned, but on the other hand the doubts about friendship itself have been cleared away. No longer do we hold back from God, fearing what we may lose in loving others. Indeed, one of the last steps in being able to see God as the all-absorbing center of our lives may be the inner assurance that we are not fighting against him by loving others deeply. Rather we find his will to be more completely in this love than even is our own. Love and trust in regard to God have made the human union more secure.

This book will be read by others who are still somewhat farther back on the road. For these it must be repeated that, although we cannot love our neighbor too much in God, the practical aspects of this love are something different. No man can do all possible good, not even all the possible good that is at hand. With this in mind we make choices based on supernatural love of self as well as the needs of our neighbor. We do not fail in love of neighbor just because we give some time to ourselves, especially such time as we are also giving to God directly. Our external activity is limited by our other duties, including those to God and to ourselves, and by our strength. This includes spiritual strength; we can unwisely move into situations for which we do not have the grace.

Not all the saints by any means seem to have entered into a close spiritual relationship with members of the opposite sex. Thus we may surely say that it is not required even though much claim is made for close association in order to reach full maturity. Providentially the Catholic religion (as well as certain other Christian denominations) provides us with other means for such fulfillment in ways that will call forth our highest development and avoid dangers which some seem to fancy do not exist. For men there is the Blessed Virgin and a choice of many women saints. For women there is the supreme love which all must give to the God-man which, for them importantly, includes his sacred humanity as well. Of course there are many male saints also.

Spiritual friendships are always a matter of personal vocation. The evidence of such a vocation, however, is not discerned by strong attraction so much as by sustained spiritual and moral fruits of the friendship. Love of God is a deeper and even a more natural necessity than the love for anyone else.

The division of time given to God and neighbor depends on vocation. This division is something admittedly hard to discern in practice. Obviously God does not want all men to dedicate themselves principally to helping their neighbor, or he would not make it impossible for some to do so. Nor would his Church so definitely and strongly approve the contemplative religious orders. Yet surely not all whom he calls to a principally contemplative vocation are called to live behind cloistered walls.

The imperative emphasis of the commandment itself is disturbing: to love one's neighbor *as oneself*, or as Christ loved this neighbor or has loved us. However, since no one man or woman can imitate the totality of Christ perfectly, we are called in different degrees to imitate various aspects of his personality and life. Thus some of us are called more to works than to contemplation, and at various periods in our life we may be called to one more than to another.

The second great commandment, urgent and universal though it is, is subordinate to the first. It commands us to love others as we love ourselves, but it presumes a correct love for ourselves in proposing this model. We can ask, then, whether we would be loving ourselves correctly if we objected to neighbors not giving time to some of our lesser needs because he was giving time, even much time, to God? In loving ourselves correctly, we must acknowledge the right of God to be loved first, totally, and if he so will it, loved relatively exclusively in portioning our time and energy.

We cannot exempt ourselves from external works merely because they are difficult in one way or another. Otherwise we would fail in the heroic degree of this virtue of love of neighbor. God does not usually have work for us far afield; most often we will be able to reach out and touch it, as with the normal duties of our state in life. It is probably true that our own surroundings will usually have enough of difficult love of neighbor to accomplish this heroic degree, even if God has no other work for us. We do not have to cross oceans to forgive those who have injured us. We do not have to search hot jungles for people who need something we can give. We always have occasions to raise above envy, jealousy, and discord. Even when we must disagree with another to the depths of our soul, we must still find room in our heart for him. Spiritual perfection is made of things like these; indeed they are a necessary condition, not only of the perfect man or woman, but also of the apostle either of the word or of charity.

Everyone who loves God has a usefulness in the world by that very fact. Because of such love God sends his blessings upon a needy, forgetful, and negligent humanity. Because of this love he holds back his punishments. Sodom would have been spared if Abraham had been able to find only ten just men living there (Gn 18:10). A condition of the destruction of the world is that "love in most men will grow cold" (Mt 24:12). God often has a more recognizable usefulness for those who love him exceedingly: he never lets his friends forget that he has other friends, and that these have needs.

It is when our lives approach the perfection of Christ that we become the completely true apostles. Any apostle that has less than the profound purpose of giving all things to God, must necessarily be diminished by giving to self or to others in ways not according to God's will and not leading to him. Since spiritual perfection does not mean the exclusive contemplation of God, there is no reason that ordinary apostles should not want to be perfect in order to be better apostles. Only then can they be really efficient channels of grace. Only then will there be nothing in them to obstruct or spoil the work of God.

Even if our work is not given success or only a part of the success we had hoped for, we lose nothing. The love of God which has been the source and end of our work is not lost; it is even increased. Further, in the mysterious and hidden purposes of God our failure will have meant a great gain for our neighbor, a neighbor we may never see in this world, but loved and suffered for by Christ just the same. For the man who loves, everything has a purpose, even failure.

A person at the summit of the spiritual life may find life very busy. St. Dominic died in the labor of building an order he had barely founded. Surely the sainted popes also fit this description as do St. John of the Cross and St. Teresa of Avila. But others will find that the call upon their time and energy is less. They will learn to use the ever widening amount of time and solitude for the purpose of living with God. This situation can come about, as we have said, because of old age or sickness, or it can come because God so wills it in other clearly indicated ways. But none of these people are outside the great and practical love of neighbor. Even when no burdens are placed on them through circumstances, they still do immense good to their neighbor, more than many active people, the same good which the Church praises in the hidden apostolate of the purely contemplative orders (Vatican II, *Decree on the Appropriate Renewal of Religious Life*, no. 7).

God is to be loved and praised for what he is in himself. He must be loved first because he alone is worthy of that kind of love. He cannot become a means to any purpose, even the sublime purpose of helping others. He alone is to be loved with the whole heart, mind, soul, and strength. The man or woman in the way of spiritual perfection sees this clearly. Thus when we speak of our love and praise of God having an effect for our neighbor, we must understand that it will have this only when it is directed to God for himself. Otherwise it would not be an acceptable kind of friendship with God. When our love for him reaches out directly to him, then the same love moves him toward our neighbor far more than if we were to do all things for others with great reaching out to others.

Great burdens of activity are often placed upon the perfect person despite the desire to be with God, and despite the desire to be dissolved and be with Christ, a desire so great that perhaps there is need to be immersed in activity in order to be distracted from it. Sometimes in particular cases also, God may have another reason for allowing good works to become a part of the life of someone very close to him. This has to do with a personal psychological condition. Not all minds have the strength to face a continuous meeting with the divine. In such confrontation, they may turn in on themselves too much, and this will be too great a strain over the long period. In other cases the defect may be spiritual, a deep potentiality toward pride even as it was in the perfect man, our father Adam. These would find themselves proud even in the midst of God's continual giving of love. And so for reasons which are personal to some of us, he sometimes fills in the spaces of time with works that are useful, even if not of the highest.

We must not be surprised that a perfect person will have such basic imperfection that God must fill in non-contemplative work in order not to upset the mind. We must again recall that by perfection we mean only the relative perfection possible in this life, and for some people this is less of certain human perfections than they would like to have. In these people, indeed with everyone, ultimate perfection does not consist in becoming autonomous or independent of divine help, but in becoming more dependent, thus still growing in virtue.

The greatest of the moral virtues is prudence, and this teaches us our own God-given strengths and also the limits of them. To accept the protection of God acting through his providence, then is the highest prudence. We do not necessarily become more of a giant in order to become more perfect; we may well become smaller, as the little child our Lord offered as an example to the quarreling and ambitious apostles. To let God guide us by the hand is indeed our greatest strength, and only the perfect are strong enough, to let him do it perfectly. The importance of love and work for our neighbor does not mean that God never gives unending opportunity for the soul to be with him. He does this in some cases, and certain saints are witnesses to it, by making the Presence so strong that the soul is aware of God and external work also. These go through their days and nights living in both worlds.

There are opportunities in the lives of most of us to be with God almost exclusively. We have mentioned old age, when there is little work we can do, and ill health. Those last are sometimes not so productive of the sweetness of communion with God as we perhaps anticipate. No doubt St. Thérèse at some busy time in her earlier life envisioned what a joy it would be to be able to give her heart continually to prayer. If she had any such human and understandable illusions, they were wrecked in the darkness which came upon her when she had enormously more time to give to prayer as an invalid. But these occasions surely do arise. St. Paul was in prison at the end of his life and there are innumerable others of the saints whose sickbed or deathbed seems to have been a dim but overwhelming foretaste of the joys of heaven. God knows what he is about in each case. We can only take from him what he gives. All the more reason not to make definite plans or demands that will require time and effort to break down. To live and love in each moment is the best preparation for the love of the last moments, whatever kind of love will then be given to us or asked of us.

Chapter 13

LIVING WITH GOD

If we do not allow ourselves to be dazzled or discouraged by descriptions of transforming union submerged in allegory and metaphor, we will more easily understand its true and precise characteristics. We have already seen some of these, and it is not our intention here to discuss all of them. Each individual will develop them according to the development of the self as designed and given by God. The spiritual life now is not a search for new conquests, or for new areas of perfection. The soul, having found itself and its spiritual way, is like a painting almost completed. Everything is where it should be; the design on the canvas matches the design in the artist's mind. There remain only the final touches to bring out emphasis here and the color there. These refinements are gently made, no longer any blotting out of whole portions of the canvas for a new start. The soul is at rest in the hands of God; now more than at any previous time it is confident that God loves it quite as it is.

The delicate balance between true love of self and true humility is now easier to maintain. What some of the saints have so often called a contempt or mistrust of self is quite easily held in the psyche along with the overflowing results of the gifts of grace. Thus, we are not so likely to become depressed by our faults or blinded by our gifts. Although we may even recognize ourselves to be in the seventh mansion, so to speak, we know deeply that but for God we would not even be in the first. And we do not give up our watchfulness, now that we are in the seventh. Indeed, in many ways it is greater than when we were in the first.

Direction by the Holy Spirit requires humility in a high degree; otherwise we could not be trusted with the full measure of God's guidance. The pollution of pride would spoil some of his best graces. This high degree of humility is the heroic degree, the same degree that is required of all virtues before we are joined to God in the fullness of the transforming union. This degree is patiently won under the almost endless trials along the way and by much prayer for so unpalatable a virtue.

The heroic degree must not be confused with an excessive degree (although what will seem excessive at one step of the way may not be so at another). For instance, we are told to turn the other cheek. Yet our Lord did not always do so. On one occasion he asked, "Why do you strike me?" (Jn 18:23). A higher value was present at the moment, the establishing both of his innocence and the prejudice of his captors and judges. Later when this was no longer relevant, he allowed himself to be struck unto death, so to speak, without protest.

Similarly, the heroic degree of humility is particularly exemplified in the forgiveness of injury. To this we may apply the same principles as above. Even with injuries done to the perfect man or woman, respect for the higher value sometimes requires that action be taken against the evil-doer, as when it involves the honor of God or the good of our neighbor, including the unjust man himself. Humility in the heroic degree is always ruled by another virtue in the heroic degree, and this virtue is holy prudence.

By now it should be obvious that the sanctity by which we enter into the transforming union is not to be thought of as being necessarily rapt to the third heaven, but rather having the feet firmly on this earth. Thus, prudence, although it rarely comes into the consideration of higher sanctity, is an essential element, at least on those many occasions when God guides our ordinary lives by ordinary means and not by the higher manner of the gift of counsel.

We can easily exaggerate the area in which we may expect the Holy Spirit to operate through the gift. But even when he does, the norms of holy prudence will be a guard against illusion, from which no man may be certain that he is free. And even when the movement of the Holy Spirit through the gift is authentic, holy prudence will guide us in many of the practical details that this guidance through the gift does not cover.

Holy prudence helps us keep the line between the heroic and the foolhardy, and sometimes, because of their close similarity, the line is very thin. The difference between them is made more difficult in some cases because as the virtues grow, the mean or norm of what is truly virtuous becomes higher. Thus a man who finds that he must be very careful about food and rest in the beginning of his spiritual life may discover a greater leeway later. But on the other hand he may not.

Humility is likewise joined to hope. We see our sins and past failures. These never stop being a source of our own abasement, especially since we know that without God we could be much worse, instead of close to him as we are. But the same sins give us hope because we see what he did for us when we were farther from him, and so with greater confidence we expect more from him now. We must not be surprised that the perfect man needs such considerations to help him. God insists on using the evil to bring about a greater good. Similarly, trials which show our weakness can be permitted not only as a source of merit for the perfect man, but also for his needed humiliation. Even St. Paul needed them in order to maintain humility. "And to keep me from being too elated by the abundance of revelation, a thorn was given me in the flesh, a messenger of Satan to harrass me, to keep me from being too elated" (2 Cor 12:7).

There is no virtue that cannot become heroic; even the most ordinary fulfillment of our duties can become heroic because of circumstances. We do not have to be burned at the stake in order to have the virtue of fortitude in a heroic degree. God will always provide occasions for heroic endurance or heroic action; we will never be left without the means to follow Christ more closely.

Fortitude, of course, is closely allied to hope. In some cases it may be heroic principally because it is depending on a hope that is heroic. And this hope may at times seem to be a hope without much hope. The hope in the soul of St. Thérèse in her last illness was not an exuberant hope, a hope filled with confident emotional joy. Instead her hope was a darkness like her faith and love. But this does not mean that her hope was unstable; rather it means that the state of heroic hope, instead of being a placid flow of constant assurance from the Holy Spirit, may be assaulted by severe temptations. And like any virtue it becomes more heroic because of them. It is not necessarily a state filled with a consoling certainty that is almost knowledge rather than hope—the image we often get of higher sanctity. But on the other hand, because God is free, it can also be that kind of hope.

This vivid kind of hope is based on the close, vivid contemplative union that God grants to some men and women in this later period of the spiritual life. They almost look upon the face of God. During this prayer of oneness they are so full of trust that no shadow of doubt can cross their minds. This is of course the same as the theological virtue of hope. The difference now is that it is experienced almost tangibly in experiencing God.

Hope is built on faith but heroic hope flows also from love, especially the love of friendship by which we want God's good rather than our own. In our love we are content if his will is done; nothing else matters very much because in love we can easily trust that will. And we know that his ultimate purposes, no matter what they are, will come about infallibly. We pray and find peace in praying that his will, the most merciful will he can bring to the situation, will be accomplished for ourselves and those with whom we are concerned. Love of him allows no doubt of him.

Love also deepens and broadens the understanding between friends, and so we will not trust God in the same way for all things. The heroic degree does not mean that we will serenely trust that God will bring about everything we would like, not only our personal wishes but even what we would want for the souls of others or for the Church in the world. St. Catherine of Siena had much discussion with God over the damnation of souls, and she desired to be a lid over the mouth of hell—all in great anguish and without achieving her desires. Even in the higher spiritual life our asking must be conditional upon the unseen wisdom of God whose ways are not always our own.

Under the influence of the gifts of the Holy Spirit we may

indeed come to understand what is God's will in an individual case, and thus trust for the outcome serenely without fear from obstacles which may be very great. But lacking this divinely given assurance, we have no way of knowing whether God intends to bring success for a given case or for the Church in the world. On one hand, it is impossible to trust the goodness and omnipotence of God too much, but on the other hand, we don't know the mind and will of God completely and, in a given situation, perhaps not at all. This is especially true in regard to his permissive will. And so our trust cannot center upon such indeterminables with the same intensity as it does in regard to God's goodness itself as the object of hope. We could even stray into excess by hoping too stubbornly in what is not his will, and this would not be the heroic degree of trust. Our heroism lies in our absolute and loving acceptance of his will, whatever the future may reveal it to be. But this, although there may be a basic serenity about it, may also be accompanied by much anguish, even in the perfect man or woman. As St. Paul cried out, "There is my daily preoccupation: my anxiety for all the churches. . . . When any man is made to fall, I am tortured" (2 Cor 11:28, 29).

Anguish does not basically affect our trust. Some such deep suffering is demanded of us for the realization of God's purposes. Calm always returns, especially when God is close to us. In our love we cannot doubt, even when his permissive will appears to be against all we would desire for others and for ourselves. We thus become more the ideal of perfect childhood. Despite his sometimes persistent delays or refusals, we confidently expect God to be a companion in the solution of our problems. Even when we are at a distance from them, he will be working out their solution, perhaps in ways of which we may not now be aware.

This all embracing trust, which is an essential condition of that childhood which will make us the greater in the kingdom of heaven, often comes at a time when the human being is, from a natural point of view, much weaker than formerly. A weakened physical condition, a psychological tiredness from the never ending battles with life, the natural loss of enthusiasm which comes from being deprived of so many sources of natural motivation through purification, even the greater awareness of weakness as exposed through the Dark Night—all this can leave a man with much less feeling of strength and well-being than when he was much farther from his goal, much less dear to God. But compensatory strength comes from expecting the strength of God to be with him at all times when it is needed. Like St. Paul he can now live with his weakness so that the strength coming from the merits of Christ may be with him, not as a permanent torrent that exalts him triumphantly on the crest of the wave, but something which even in his weakness he knows will be with him in his needs. Thus, a poor human, he finds peace in the love and power of God.

Contrary to what we would expect of the transforming union if we only concentrated on the delights of higher prayer, the life of the perfect man or woman is not a stranger to all kinds of suffering. Not only is this suffering physical but it can be mental and spiritual also. It can come from obstacles to our work or to God's purposes in the world, or it can be more personal in the misunderstandings, insults, and perhaps calumnies, coming even from good people. The internal troubles, however, which once were so deeply disturbing, are generally over, but here again we cannot limit the free will of God. Besides St. Paul and St. Thérèse of Lisieux there are St. Alphonsus Liguori and St. Paul of the Cross as examples of whom God asks deep interior suffering even after their own purification has been accomplished. This surely is asked as a reparation for others and as a sacrifice for the good of the Church, as well as for reasons more basic (the greater glory of God) and more personal (the increase of love and merit for the one suffering).

On the other hand, so much is suffering a condition of the saints that some of them seem to extol it as if it were the supreme joy of life. Quite truly this is not a suffering for its own sake, but rather a painful experience accepted for the love of God and for the good of others. Their general attitude can be given in the words of St. Augustine: "When one loves, one does not suffer, or if one does, the very suffering is loved." And St. Thérèse says at the other end of the Christian era, "Do not be sad about me. I have reached the point of not being able to suffer any more because suffering is so sweet to me."

Such testimonies are too frequent to be dismissed as flashes of the fervor of the moment. Surely, to love for his sake what God sends or permits, must be a characteristic of the soul closely united to him in love. There is a danger, however, of going from this love of suffering to the insistence that *joy* in suffering is an inseparable and constant characteristic of the transforming union. Indeed St. Teresa of Avila notes that the great desire for suffering now changes into wanting God's will more than any suffering (See *Interior Castle*, VII, 3).

For clarification we can distinguish between an emotional joy and an essential joy, a certain joy of the will. There can be joy in the will without a corresponding feeling in the emotions. By a joy in the will we make ourselves joyful in attitude of mind by the considerations we apply to it, such as the love we have for God, the good that our sufferings do for others, or the joy we will have in heaven because of them. St. Paul outlines one method of doing this: "We rejoice in our sufferings, knowing that suffering produces endurance, and endurance produces character, and character produces hope, and hope does not disappoint us, because God's love has been poured into our hearts through the Holy Spirit which has been given to us" (Rm 5:3).

Spiritual joy differs from peace in that it is a more positive going out toward God whereas inner peace is more a resting in him. We may at times, even frequently, make ourselves show this joy exteriorly, not because of spontaneous feeling, but again by willing it. Surely at times we will also be moved toward emotional joy in our sufferings, and this is more apt to happen while in the closely felt presence of God.

We must not place upon the state of perfection the obligation that we feel emotionally joyful all the time. Certain situations, even outside of suffering, will call for other expressions besides joy, situations where a serious demeanor would be more appropriate than a perpetual or a forced smile. We can hardly imagine Mary at the foot of the cross with a smile on her face and joy flowing from her heart. It should also be noted that St. Thérèse of Lisieux had very little of emotional joy in her last sufferings, and that our Lord seems to have had none of it in his. Probably the examples of the saints in whom joy in suffering is especially noted were those who were given "the most" and "the highest." It is most interesting to note that our Lord did not give himself "the most" and "the highest" in some categories.

Joy in the will is based upon hope and love. As to hope, the spiritual motives for joy imply God's infallible ability to bring a greater good out of any evil which may happen in the Church, in the world, and even from the evil of our own sinfulness and unworthiness. But most of all joy flows from love. One might find peace through trust without much love, but joy is the fruit of great love. We are joyful simply because we love God so much, and this joy extends to his will under most circumstances, even his permissive will.

There are, of course, certain sufferings from which joy can come more readily (e.g., Ac 5:41). These are predominantly physical sufferings or bad treatment by others. But even here we have St. Bernadette asking for a pain-killer in her last illness. Trials that we can see as designed for our purification or growth in virtue are also easily a cause for joy; they mean more of the Beloved and often are a means of greater inner freedom. Furthermore, since these sufferings do not profit us alone but are a means of help and salvation through and with Christ for many others, they are for this reason also a cause of joy. Thus, not in every instance but in general we find an essential joy if we love enough, a joy not always in the things themselves but always in a loving God who gave his Son to suffering and death because of love.

The joy of the perfect man or woman comes from God more than from persons or things. This is not to say that they have lost their power to delight, but rather that we tend to see God in all and through all. Since he is the Beloved who has increasingly filled the whole of life, we tend to see whatever happens principally in relation to him and to his love. Love of God is the secret of joy. When his presence is closely felt, he alone is the reason for the deepest content or joy. He by himself can turn any darkness into light. And even when he is not in evidence by his felt presence, love still sees all from his point of view—not always with blindingly clear insight but at least with a faith and trust that do not fail.

Indeed in one respect, the more difficult a thing is, the greater is the call for supernatural joy. It is true that both pleasant events and crosses come from God in some way. The pleasant event, however, has an affinity for joy in its own right whereas the cross principally points to the will of God as the cause for joy. Our perfect will finds it a joy because it gives God a more exclusive and greater love, as well as greater glory. More than any other, the perfect man or woman understands what was sung long ago: "Whom have I in heaven but thee? And there is nothing on earth I desire besides thee" (Ps 72:25).

On the other hand, there are certain kinds of suffering which ought not to make us joyful. It would be hard to imagine St. Augustine being joyful in the midst of the siege of his city by the Vandals, or rejoicing over its capture if he had lived to see that. St. Thérèse would not be expected to be joyful if one of her sisters had left the convent for a life of sin. Sufferings, moreover, because of injustice to our neighbor ought not to make us joyful. Since those close to God are more sensitive in all these areas, being a saint is not always a happy business, but those around him seldom know it.

Not always at every moment, but always after sufficient reflection, the perfect soul can find a way or a reason to rejoice, at least with essential joy. In this way, the human mind of Christ was able to rejoice in the good effects of his death and sufferings, including his desolation in the garden and on the cross. He was able to do this with a spiritual joy in the highest part of his soul even at the time of his sufferings, and with his whole heart and soul afterwards. The same is true for us, as he promised: "You will grieve for a time but your grief will be turned into joy" (Jn 16:20). As we grow closer to God, our anxieties are quieted by being able to rejoice that God's ultimate will for some greater good, will be accomplished even if our own desires and plans will not.

Sadness is a passion put into our psyche by God. Thus it is a legitimate part of human nature and we must not expect that it will be destroyed by grace. There are situations in which it would be wrong not to be sad, even when we love God very much—or even more because of it. We would not expect St. Catherine of Siena to be joyful over the state of the Church in her lifetime, and her letters show that she was not. St. Paul who urges the Philippians always to rejoice (4:4) found it impossible himself. "When I arrived in Macedonia I was restless and exhausted. I was under all kinds of stress—quarrels with others and fears within myself" (2 Cor 7:5).

The absence of constant joy in St. Paul, instead of being contrary to the experience of our great mystical writers, is used by St. Teresa to describe her state of soul after her ecstasies and raptures. "To have to return, to have to look at this farce of a life and see how ill-organized it is, to spend the time in meeting the needs of the body, in sleeping and eating . . . wearied by everything . . . cannot run away . . . sees itself chained and captive . . . it is then that the soul feels most keenly the imprisonment into which we are led by our bodies and the misery of life. It understands why St. Paul besought God to deliver him from it" (Rm 7:24; St. Teresa, *Life*, ch. 12).

God, however, had many ways of restoring her to peace and joy. One way was to remember past spiritual favors from him whenever she felt "miserable" (*Interior Castle*, VI, 5). Nor does this peace come always and only by supernatural means. St. Paul's distress in Macedonia was also not for long: "But God who gives heart to those who are low in spirit, gave me strength with the arrival of Titus . . . not only by his arrival . . . for he reported your longing, your grief, and your ardent concern for me, so that my joy is greater still" (2 Cor 7:5, 6, 7).

Is it too much to say that the life of the transforming union is not all joy, not all suffering? Like the rest of life, it is an undulation between the two, though still with a peace that can say when the trial is over, "I am overflowing with gladness in spite of all our suffering" (ib. v. 4).

If we did not have the example of Christ, we might imagine that the life of the perfect is a life of perfect calm: a man is not really a saint if he is sometimes sad. But on the other hand, Christ is the way and the life. Who would meet with the sinfulness of bad priests or lax religious and not feel a sadness? Who would go through the agonies of a Church suffering from without, or worse, suffering from within, and not be like Christ in the Garden or abandoned on the cross? Thus the words of the mystics about joy in suffering must be applied with understanding of our human situation. God's intimate presence, however, can compensate and can make us forget, giving us a foretaste of heaven even on a sinful earth and above a blaspheming hell. But this is not done at all times, unless God in his freedom were to extend this state to all the hours of life. Perhaps he will do so for some of us shortly before the end.

PART III

TRANSFORMATION
THROUGH PRAYER

Chapter 14

THE MYSTICAL STATE

The unfortunate ability of nomenclature to get in the way of reality is never more apparent than in the use of the word "mystic" and its derivatives. So much does it seem to imply someone more than merely human living in a remote cloister, in a lonely cave, in a rock, or in a Buddhist lamasery that we have tried to avoid using it in a book which is written for ordinary people in ordinary situations. Yet the term, sounding esoteric, surely describes something which can happen to ordinary people: the presence of God given in prayer, although isolated mystical acts, do not put one into the mystical state.

The term "mystic" is also used in a sense related to the truly extraordinary phenomena such as visions or prophecies, and of these we shall not be speaking in this book. But the presence of God in all degrees of contemplative prayer is not basically beyond the ordinary way, as we shall see later.

In our treatment of contemplative prayer as the consistently important, or seeming constitutive element of the mystical state, we are aware of the generally solid opinion of some others who see the gifts of the Holy Spirit as the constitutive element of this state. We do not wish to seem in opposition to this position, and therefore a few words in explanation of our treatment may be a clarification.

It seems that any opposition between contemplative prayer and the gifts as the constitutive element of the mystical state is an opposition of a part to the whole, of a more manifest or prominent part to the less manifest or prominent whole. The part is contemplative prayer, which is a manifestation principally of the gifts of wisdom and understanding, and the whole is all seven gifts. In our mind this is not a real opposition, because we do not intend to exclude the manifestations of the other five gifts, nor the other manifestations of the gifts of wisdom and understanding. We see concentration on contemplative prayer only as an emphasis.

Contemplative prayer is generally agreed not to exceed the dimensions of the virtue of faith but rather is an impression and quasi-experimental manifestation of the God we know by faith. This comes principally, as we have said, through the actuation of the gifts of wisdom and understanding. This being so, there is no theological reason for selecting contemplative prayer in place of the gifts as a whole, because all the gifts grow simultaneously with sanctifying grace in the soul. The actuation of one gift rather than another, however, depends in general on the free will of God acting through our personal vocation. Although all the gifts radically grow at the same rate, they are not actuated by the Holy Spirit in an equal proportion. Thus, St. Thérèse of Lisieux had relatively little contemplative prayer as compared to some other saints, but much of the gift of piety toward God as Father.

Therefore it is because of reasons more practical than theological that contemplative prayer is emphasized in discussing the mystical state. The practical reasons which occur to us are the following:

First of all, the traditional Christian understanding of mysticism always emphasizes an intimate relationship with God. At times this involves extraordinary manifestations beyond the definition either of contemplative prayer or of the gifts of the Holy Spirit. Always, however, there is this intimate relationship which also implies some personal spiritual contact initiated by God. While the actuation of any of the gifts of the Holy Spirit depends on the initiative of the Holy Spirt, most of them do not imply the personal oneness of the loving knowledge that come through contemplative prayer. Therefore, contemplative prayer most fittingly is emphasized in any treatment of the mystical state.

Secondly, since the divine presence is more immediately

known than many of the other actuations of the gifts, it is a more convenient criterion of the mystical state. It requires less analysis (and analysis is always detrimental to mystical experience). Thus, for example, it is sometimes difficult in practice to discern whether a given decision is from the gift of counsel or from the virtue of holy prudence. Or whether an insight into a doctrine of Christianity is a simple illumination of the virtue of faith, such as comes to all men who are concerned with knowledge, or is it an actuation of the gift of understanding. In short, is there any practical way by which we can come upon the transcendental element, which is characteristic of the gifts, and come upon it as simply as we do with the felt presence of God?

Finally, this emphasis seems to have the support of a common consensus in the Church. For instance, if the Holy Spirit in his freedom were to emphasize in some saint the gift of fortitude, but without much discernable grace of contemplative prayer, this man or woman would not be called a mystic. Likewise if a saint were able to solve intricate personal problems for others so that we could deduce the presence of the gift of counsel, but again with no great evidence of contemplative prayer, we would not term him a mystic. Yet some recluse who spent long hours in ecstatic prayer, but gave no great evidence of the other gifts than what might be theologically assumed because of strong virtues, would be called a mystic. Thus we will continue to follow this practice, while not excluding the objective reality of the necessity and presence of the gifts in a rich and varied individual manifestation.

In beginning our discussion of prayer, we must again put unitive prayer into its proper perspective with the rest of the spiritual life, of which even the highest contemplative prayer is only a part. Our basic relationship with God is not whether we have proceeded beyond this or that grade of prayer, but how close we are in friendship. This friendship, as we have said, is basically the state of sanctifying grace, or the virtue of love or charity deep in the soul. In this the mystic is no different from the rest of men in the same state of grace of love. As such he cannot claim a greater degree of the friendship of God than someone who is not a mystic, because there have been saints in grace who have had very little of contemplative prayer. Rather the difference is only that he is given a certain conscious intimacy with the friend.

Since this intimacy is with God himself, we cannot help but think of it as a reward, a foretaste of the eternal vision. And in some sense it is, although experience is often to the contrary: not a reward but a preparation for trials perhaps severe or prolonged just around the corner. Even though this is not universally true either, it is true often enough to give us the impression that this kind of prayer can easily be considered a special help from God as well as a sign of his friendship. But then, the cross is also a sign of his friendship. In any case it is a matter of the free choice of God, which choice is our personal, individual vocation. God draws some men more in this way than he draws others. Their natural bent, even to the physical dispositions of temperament, seem to be factors resulting from his choice. We do not make our vocation in this regard; rather we spend our lives seeking the fullness of it.

This choice on the part of God, however, does not mean that humanity is artificially divided into contemplatives and non-contemplatives. The choice is a matter of degree; all human nature has a potentiality to follow the call of the Creator, and thus at any time can be given the insight of his presence which is contemplative prayer. Yet some men, and we can see this clearly in the different saints, have a definitely contemplative bent while others have not. And of course some men are so well gifted that they have both great ability for contemplative prayer and great power of activity. St. Paul comes to mind first, and we immediately also think of men like St. Dominic and St. Francis of Assisi, and of women like St. Catherine of Siena and St. Teresa of Avila. Pages could be filled with many such names.

This psychological or physical bent toward contemplation, however, is not restricted to the saints, nor is it restricted to Catholics. The disposition is there by nature under God's universal providence, and thus there are also people outside the faith who are more disposed to be receptive to this prayer than some who have the true faith. There is no reason why God cannot admit some of these into the enjoyment of his presence, and it is a fact that he has sometimes done so.

We must by no means think that the closely felt presence of God was something discovered only in the age of the great mystics. It is not an unreasonable surmise that it was an experience known in far earlier times. Indeed from the very earliest eras of man, just as in the remotest tribes ever since, conceivably this presence has been given to at least a few in order to keep alive the belief in a supreme and transcendent being, however distorted may have been some of the religious structures into which it was received.

Probably few men, if any, have equaled in vividness what Moses experienced on Mt. Sinai when he asked God to show him his glory (Ex 34:18-23). And we cannot imagine how the love verses of many of the psalms came to be, unless we also understand that David and the other writers felt the same presence that the great mystics write about and that we can experience today. Nor would it be prudent to interpret the reaches of St. Paul's love as only blind faith when he speaks in such terms as "that you, being rooted and grounded in love, may have the power to comprehend with all the saints what is the breadth and length and height and depth, and to know the love of Christ which surpasses knowledge; and that you may be filled with all the fullness of God" (Ep 3:17-19). Thus, we do not really need a training course in contemplative prayer, in order to understand that this is God who is now close to us, and to know how to respond.

As for those outside the Chosen People and the true faith, we should expect a high frequency of contemplative prayer among the many holy men and women of the Eastern Orthodox and similar religions. We should expect this since their faith differs from the whole faith on relatively few points, and also because they have the true priesthood and sacraments, as well as the ascetical tradition once shared by all of us.

Surely no one would expect that the Protestant and the other more recent churches would be without the manifestation of God's presence in some individuals. But in their case it is difficult to make even the general statements we are making here, because of a lack of unity of belief and practice. Some claim the personal action of the Holy Spirit in what surely is an exaggerated degree. Others do not look for any manifestation of God, and seemingly would regard mysticism with suspicion. Not that the expression "mystic" itself does not leave room for well-grounded fears in all religions. So loosely is the word sometimes applied that many are called by that name who have little relationship to the presence of God, but are so called just because they are religious, somewhat distant, and a little odd.

But to limit ourselves to what we understand here by a mystic, our separated brethren among these sects (and also those sincere people who profess no formal religion) run special dangers. They lack a tradition in which the distilled experience of the Christian centuries more easily points out to a sincere seeker his direction as well as the perils along the road. We find here people who, because of their personal bent of temperament or the influence of (or despair over) their environment and times, will desire the taste of mystical experience. None of this excludes the grace of God, surely for the Spirit ever breathes where he will.

Their interest in mysticism, however, generally has not come to them from the bottom up, that is from love of God on a lower plane and from thence on to something more. It is more likely that they have become interested in the spiritual life by having read deeply in the mystical literature, in itself a good thing. The danger in this for anyone, for that matter, is that they will choose this way for self-development or self-expression, instead of the love of God. A telltale characteristic is often the desire for the heights without traversing the painful footsteps of the virtues. Pride is apt not to be very far from the surface, even when they are naturally good by their temperament or environment, or even by a rigorous asceticism.

But when we consider that God loves his children despite a poor start and mixed motives, which many with the whole faith often share, who is to say that he will not at times eventually come to these people? If the best of men are poor, in our universal need, why should he be said to avoid those who are poorer, even in some cases very much poorer?

Perhaps to a lesser extent, but still with certainty we must expect this infused presence of God among the holy Jews and Moslems. These do not have the knowledge through Christ of the intense personal love that God has for each man, and are consequently the poorer for it. But nevertheless, because of their belief in the one true God whom they meet in sincere faith, it is not surprising that he meets some of them in his presence of love.

We do not of course say that every claim to mystical experience is valid among all these, any more than we would admit every such claim from our own. We surely expect, and do find, that the kind of mystical experience we are talking about comes more abundantly in those who love God under the guidance of the whole faith and with the help of the sacraments. Of those outside, some religions generally discourage the kind of attitude which would induce a man to prepare for contact with God. Such are the Jews and Moslems, with very notable exceptions both in men and in movements. Others such as the Hindus and Buddhists surely do not discourage such natural preparation. In fact, it is an essential part of these religions in their higher forms.

In these religions of the Far East, however, the high moral teaching and the ascetical discipline, as in the case of yoga, can give this mysticism a recommendation among us which is beyond its power to fulfill. It is true that the physical disciplines can be brought under the roof of the faith and thus have a usefulness limited to a few. These disciplines can, for instance, calm the restlessness of the body which is sometimes an obstacle to the quiet needed for the contemplation of God.

God's presence often brings its own sense of quiet. But this physically and psychologically imposed quiet cannot bring the infused or given presence of God. This must be infused or given. At best such physical disciplines can bring about acquired contemplation which is something entirely different, though quite truly of no small benefit.

Nevertheless, these real but limited benefits of Eastern mysticism are marred by theological teaching which is more likely to turn us away from the true God than lead us toward him. The winding road of doctrine will tend to keep us from the consciousness of the Other and will end up with the consciousness either of an emptiness or of a consciousness of the self which can become an unconscious illusion of transcendency or of an absolute. This is not to say that none of these men have found the true God. Knowing God for what he is, a Father who loves all his children, we should expect that he will in some cases show himself despite the deficiencies of doctrine, even as the truth itself shines out here and there in these doctrines.

One cannot therefore argue from the genuineness of an individual experience back to a genuineness of doctrine. Doctrine is established on its own grounds and according to its own principles. The most that can be said is that we expect and do find a closer relationship with God, and among great numbers, when there is true doctrine and the great means of grace such as the Mass and the sacraments. Even great sincerity has enormous difficulty in compensating for a lack of these.

Contemplative prayer, even the highest, has far greater limitations than one would expect who has not experienced it. In itself it teaches us little we do not know; we know about God and his love by faith, and this is also the principal message of contemplative prayer. If more enlightenment is given, it is likely to be a matter of the extraordinary: revelation and not contemplative prayer. Likewise this prayer does not directly help us to solve our problems. It does, however, give us a sense of trust. Our problems will usually be solved elsewhere by God and ourselves, but this prayer can greatly support our inner security and this means peace.

Contemplative prayer also does not directly teach us how to be better; what it does is to make us want to be better, and it can be an occasion of the increase of sanctifying grace and the infused virtues, besides bringing many actual graces. Rather than a given experience of God being a proof of sanctity, it is the goodness of life which is the proof of the prayer—generally anyhow, because this prayer is a means of grace, and as a means of grace it can be given to anyone, even to sinners, under the freedom of God. In such cases, however, it will tend to show results in the growth of the virtues, unless it is absolutely being rejected or submerged by a life contrary to God who is calling.

Against those who deny all possible experience of God, who they say might not be there anyway, and who attribute these feelings to an unhealthy subjectivism, we principally point to the effects. Since effects flow from their cause, then the authentic mystic should be easily detected by the results, especially in his personal development but also in his external activity. Subjectivism, because it is an unhealthy psychological condition, should easily show itself, and there are enough unstable religious fanatics to show this difference.

To ask that the experience prove itself to another *by itself*, however, is usually asking too much of it. It is true that St. Teresa tells us again and again that no power on earth could produce such impressions on the soul, and in greater or less degree the same can be affirmed by everyone who has had experience of God with any intensity. For one outside the experience, the external criteria of advance in the virtues must usually be demanded as proof, not to speak of the need of these criteria for the mystic as well. For unfortunately the same subjective certainty is also held by the false mystic or the fanatic, and perhaps even more so.

At times it is difficult to judge conclusively, even for the person himself. However, as he grows in experience and in the virtues of love and humility, he may receive the power to sense the difference, whether this is of God, of self, or cleverly of the devil. For instance, he learns to suspect a strong wind that seemingly has no impulse toward God and ends in a sense of emptiness, although he does not make the opposite mistake of always expecting the impression of God to last beyond the experience itself, or to be reached by reason or recalled by vivid memory afterwards. As we said, however, at times he will not be able to tell for certain, and he must press on without undue compulsion to demand a judgment. He must be content with his determination or intention to honor only the true God and to give himself to him alone. If he truly loves this God and not himself unduly as one in contact with God, he will not be long under doubt or deception.

The spiritual man must rather concentrate upon perfecting himself, for God, than upon examining the phenomena of his states of prayer. His prayer becomes secure only to the extent that his whole life becomes more perfect, not only because his weaknesses keep him from God and even tend to induce illusion, but also because the devil then has a corresponding power over him. To the extent that we have spiritual, psychological, and physical weakness, we are open to the influence of the devil. This influence can be offset by a deep and prayerful dependence upon God, even in the weakest of us. But to the extent that we give in to these weaknesses, especially when in our pride over our spiritual life we may try to become independent of God, we give the devil the power to control us.

From the necessity that the mystic produce authentic virtues, and tend toward producing them in the heroic degree as his prayer continues over a longer period, we can see that he is not someone set apart from the rest of humanity. From the tenor of some books on prayer one might receive the impression that higher prayer is sanctity or that prayer alone is sufficient to make the saint. From the lack of mention of the other and greater means of grace which are the Mass and the sacraments, one might wonder if these are not pieces of baggage to be left behind in changing trains. On the contrary, it must be noted once more that the ordinary means to reach the transforming union are basically no different from those we started with. It may seem elementary to mention this, but there is the subtle danger that having read so much about the phenomena connected with the spiritual marriage, we will unconsciously give more importance to these than the means God has established for everyone through the Church, allowing of course for God's special providence for those who do not have Mass or sacraments, or do not have them in abundance.

Not only can such concentration on phenomena, which happened to some, but not all who reached the transforming union, make us think less of the universal means of grace in the Church, but it may somehow make us unconsciously expect that this union is a work accomplished outside God's general plan for man, that is, something solely between ourselves and God, and also some-

how make it *our* work and less the work of the redeeming Christ.
Like the rest of humanity the mystic must work out his salvation.
His hands too must till the earth of the spiritual life, and his crops
must be watered by the same supernatural grace from the gratuitous redemption of Christ.

Thus the mystic is not dispensed from the obligation of following the whole gospel. He does not outgrow the humanity of the
Christ who is always the way,and becomes much more so now.
The authentic push in prayer is toward becoming more conscious
of him in the Blessed Sacrament, whether in the Mass or in the
tabernacle, and more deeply aware of what it means to be re-
deemed by him. Christ becomes more and more alive to us; more
and more do we desire to see him in the kingdom of the Father.

Another inestimable help has been given to us throughout our
spiritual journey, and this, as we would expect of the Creator, is a
woman. As mother of the human body of Christ, Mary is also the
mother of his Mystical Body, and that means that she is the
mother of each one of us, to help us grow into the full stature of
Christ. Her powerful influence is not only for the simple people
who merely want little things from God. She is eminently more
the desirous helper of those who want great things from God, who
thirstingly want God himself. As one who has experienced the
greatest closeness to him, she will understand our longing. Our
love for her grows with the love of God, and takes none away from
him. Without intruding, she is ever involved in the battles and joys
of our spirit.

The way to the divine is never divorced from the human. The
way to God is unconsciously frightening, not only because of what
we are, but also because of what God is. No matter how good and
lovable he is, he cannot stop being God who is also holiness and
majesty. The assurance which comes from the companionship of
Jesus and Mary, as well as our beloved saints and angels, is a
support which may mean the difference between full union with
God and only the approach to it.

The mystical state, implying as it does a certain union with
God in contemplative prayer, does not always or necessarily show
us how close we are to him in sanctifying grace. This more essen-

tial union is always shown, however, by what we are through actual grace. Our Lord, in enumerating those who will be very close to God, tells us that we are blessed or happy when we are poor in spirit, meek or gentle, merciful, pure in heart, desirous for peace, and filled with various kinds of suffering. To be thus blessed or happy, we must have gifts of the Holy Spirit and the virtues in this highest degree, especially the virtue that moves toward the highest, love of God and the love of man in God. By the fulfillment of words like these we shall be accepted infallibly by God as his closest friends, regardless of our amount or lack of mystical experience.

Chapter 15

EVOLUTION IN PRAYER

In order to arrive at our final spiritual perfection, we will have to learn many things about ourselves. Among these are how we can best come close to God, what we need on the way, and how we must love and use God's creation. In a personal sense these and others have been the plan for the building which is our spiritual life. And now, just because from the top of the building we are able to see above the clouds, it must not be presumed that the building is to be destroyed. Spiritually, in the way we have found life, we will probably live out our life, for we are always one thing with ourselves.

One who receives the gift of contemplative prayer does not become a disembodied spirit. He remains himself. He will have the same general personality with the same general psychological and physical factors he had before. It is to be expected that his spiritual state will be changed for the better, and often any psychological defects will be corrected under the graces which come with spiritual progress in the virtues. But he would be accurately recognized for the same person he was before being given mystical prayer.

Our Lord has told us that we can judge the tree by its fruit, and the Holy Spirit has given us an idea of what fruits to look for: "But the fruit of the Spirit is love, joy, peace, patient endurance, kindness, generosity, faith, mildness, and chastity" (Gal 5:22, 23). Such evidence of intense inner union is within our grasp by grace; it can be worked for and be obtained. Closeness to God in prayer, however, cannot be obtained so surely, and we may lose the road if we go off into the fields in search of it.

Before discussing contemplative prayer as it is usually described for this final state, it seems better to spend a short time on contemplative prayer in general, especially as it may be experienced in the first conscious states of it.

Not all prayer in the final stage of the spiritual life is necessarily prayer of the highest degree. If we do not show this, we will be guilty of isolating the transforming union on the summit of the experience of God and thus prolong the confusion about this state instead of dispelling it. By retracing some of the ground, we will see how the lower fits into the higher and how the higher forms have essential points of similarity with the lower.

For those who are reading about contemplative prayer, or contemplation, for the first time there is the need here to give a clear idea of what it is. A quotation from Alvares de Paz, a Jesuit contemporary of the two great Carmelites, will help.

> "It is a new infusion made to the mind. . . . Thus furnished and strengthened by the highest help, the mind sees God. It does not accomplish this by denying anything from him as when we say: God is good and wise. But it is by regarding the divine greatness without any admixture of anything else. . . . Certainly, O reader, when you see the light with bodily eyes, you do not arrive thereat by a comparison of ideas. You simply see the light. In the same way the soul, in the degree of contemplation, affirms nothing, attributes nothing, but in complete repose it sees God. It will be said: This is astonishing, or rather, unbelievable. I admit it is astonishing. The fact, however, is very certain" (*De Inquisitione pacis*, 3:14).

To understand contemplative prayer we must always carefully evaluate the language of metaphor. The best metaphor we have is the word "see." And yet in contemplative prayer we do not see as we ordinarily use the word. The outer senses are not a part of the prayer; in fact any visions or voices, whether external or internal, are something essentially different from contemplative prayer. Thus, we also do not see inwardly either, with the imagination or the memory. The "seeing" is done by the intellect alone, in being aware of the presence of God, but without images or voice to tell us that it is God. And yet we can be very certain of this fact.

The intellect does not go out in search of God as if we were looking up something in a book. The essential part of all contemplative prayer, from the lowest to the highest, is that it is given— "infused" is the theological word for it—given by God. It is given principally to those whose spiritual and moral life is somewhat advanced. But in God's freedom it can be denied to these and sometimes given to those who are not even beginners, given in order to draw them to a better and higher life.

Since it is given, one does not get it by merely emptying the mind of everything. Surely a spirit of habitual recollection, especially when at prayer, is more likely to be a helpful disposition and also will enable one to recognize the presence when it is faint. But the truth is that it can come at any time, any place, or under almost any circumstances, and when it comes it usually brings its own inner peace.

Some receive this presence of God easily in a quiet repose of the inner mind. (This may indicate a high disposition for it, or it may mean that the presence is very strong.) On other occasions the mind may have difficulty in keeping the required suspending of the judgment and the imagination. These faculties cannot reach the experience, and this explains why it is difficult to describe what has taken place and why the language used to describe it is very inadequate.

There is always the temptation in the life of prayer to search the books for descriptions to see whether the prayer which we experience fits this or that description. Sometimes the nomenclature is so varying and so subdivided into numerous classifications, that the investigation is more confusing than helpful. We soon learn also that we do not remember the descriptions anyway. They are learned only for the moment and then forgotten with a completeness that suggests that we are not really supposed to be much concerned about descriptions. The more we use the description to compare it with our experience, the more we will be watching ourselves. But in watching ourselves, we will be failing to look at God. Yet, looking at God is contemplative prayer.

The power of reflecting on oneself, athough one of the essential characteristics of the human species, can sometimes be destructive of this kind of prayer. In the higher forms of it, the presence of God tends to sweep self-reflection away, but in the lower forms this power remains active and sometimes can cause no little difficulty. Then, when the mind is barely able to hold on to the faint edge of the presence of God, reflection on what one is doing can get in the way of concentrating on God. Even though the comparison with seeing is very apt, it does not completely alert us to this error. Mental introspection is different from seeing. I can tell my eye that it is seeing, and I can still keep on seeing at the same time. But if I tell my mind that it is looking at God, or even tell it to go on looking at him, it is my mind telling my mind. So when I use my mind for telling, I cannot use it at the same time for experiencing God.

Contemplative prayer in general can vary, not only by way of intensity, but also by the human faculty to which it is directed. Thus, sometimes it is directed by God more to the intellect and then it is more like seeing (although there is apt to be some love also). At other times it is directed more to the will. Then the response is more completely in loving, something which should be simple to understand, because it is love. But in this experience of God, it is not easy to understand—or rather it is much more simple than any love we may have experienced, and for that reason, as well as the fact that it is God, it is more difficult for our mind to grasp. This love is more simple because in its bare essence it does not include the emotions, although in some forms of contemplative prayer the emotions may accompany it, as an overflowing from it and not a cause of it.

In contemplative prayer we learn to avoid a normal connotation of love, that love be manifested by many uttered expressions of love. Love now becomes in general a wordless love, a love experienced by simply being with God, rather than expressed in separate sentiments of love. On some occasions of this prayer our nature may want to love in a more natural manner—with words and emotions—than may be advisable at the moment. But this sometimes can have the result of destroying the prayer, especially if the presence of God is relatively faint.

To understand the difference between this kind of love and ordinary love, it may be helpful, especially in the cases of the lower forms of contemplative prayer, to look upon the prayer as a meeting, rather than as a close embrace. Since we are forced to use the language of metaphor, this describes the fainter kind of contemplative prayer, whereas the strong kind is better compared to an embrace. But even the word "meeting" is insufficient, because it is a meeting deep within us, in the most interior part of our soul which is the intellect and the will.

Even the strong act of the will, determined to have or wanting to have more of God can sometimes destroy the prayer. Here the communication of love is possible only in the quiet gentleness of meeting, rather than smothering the presence in an attempt to assert our love.

The unwise attempt to hold on to God in too natural a love, may not only come from our nature, but may also be brought on by expecting too much, because of descriptions of contemplative prayer which we may have read. God may intend here and now only a faint glimpse of himself, or it may be a clearer glance, but swift in coming and swift in going. And we must not expect to be in seventh heaven for the rest of the day just because he has come. The experience of his presence will extend throughout the day, only if he stays with us to some degree. Otherwise, we may have to practice the presence of God by our own acts of the will and be content with that. In all prayer we must approach God like unspoiled children, after the manner of children of the poor, or of primitive peoples, children who may have very little and still be content and happy.

While the most common experience of contemplative prayer is to experience God as God, there are other possibilities. These do not have to be classified as extraordinary graces, as one sometimes reads. An example is the experience of the Blessed Trinity or any one of the three divine Persons. The same can be said for the attributes of God, such as his majesty or love, which one might experience in contemplative prayer. These beliefs are all in the soul habitually by the virtue of faith, and it would seem that nothing which is known by faith, and is brought to consciousness in contemplative prayer, should be classified as extraordinary—as it would be, for instance, if Christ in a vision were to address the soul directly with some communication. Indeed, if the above opinion were true, any "felt" presence of Christ in the tabernacle or in the Eucharistic Presence after Holy Communion would have to be classified that way. But this is too common an experience to be called extraordinary.

Although there is no rigorous connection between contemplative prayer and the degree of sanctifying grace, the higher degrees of contemplative prayer fittingly express the deeper union of sanctifying grace, as the soul becomes closer and closer to God. Through contemplative prayer we are brought up against God in some conscious manner; we are even immersed in him or permeated by him, so intimate can be his presence. However, contemplative prayer is possible only when it is given, even for the perfect. There may be times when the soul is in darkness or relative darkness when it must go to God by means of acts of the mind, by the repeated words of affective prayer, or by faith.

Contemplative prayer, especially in the more intense degree, is our highest kind of love, when love is understood as expressed love. This union of soul with God does not need the many words or repeated acts as formerly, no more than does the embrace of love of husband and wife need the many words of courtship by which they learned about each other. With them now, little more is needed to express love than to give themselves to their union and to its instincts which unite body to body and soul to soul. Similarly, by merely showing himself thus clearly to us, God shows us love even though there are no words of love coming from him.

There are, of course, just as in marriage, other manifestations of love, especially those of duty and sacrifice. But between God and ourselves, when he gives this wordless invitation, then the essentially wordless offering of ourselves is the highest act of directly expressed love. The words and acts of the mind and will that may now arise, flow instinctively from love, even as in the love of marriage. Just as in marriage, not every embrace is the complete embrace. So even when this prayer is given, there are varying degrees also, and this throughout our whole life on earth. Fluctuation is our human condition of life.

This fact of fluctuation must be stressed because an impression easily derived from the literature on contemplative prayer is that there is a steady evolution from the lower forms to the higher. What is not stressed is the fact that the evolution is only general; God is free to give himself to us as he wills, and besides, we are not always equally disposed to enjoy him to the fullness of his giving on each occasion. Thus there is not only a variation in respect to one degree of prayer and another at different times of prayer, but also there can be a mixture of one with another during any one period of prayer.

Despite the evidence of some evolution in prayer we must not think that God is manifesting his presence as evidence of an increasing in the basic union of grace. It is certain that he does not necessarily do this. We have, for instance, the evident growth of grace and the virtues during the Dark Night, and yet there is no concurring increase of the manifestation of God's presence. In fact, the darkness may grow deeper. Besides, he has not shown much of his presence to some of the saints. After what seems to be the highest spiritual experiences, he has asked some of them to spend years in darkness, no doubt principally for the good of others, but also for an enormous increase of grace in their own souls. How impossible to categorize the action of God by predicting what will happen to the individual soul! Only in general, and in the abstract can we speak of an evolution.

One of the important steps in the evolution of contemplative prayer concerns the prayer of union. In a sense this takes us back to the very beginnings of our life of prayer, when we perhaps found it easy to reach God by many words, by reasoned considerations, and perhaps also by the outpouring of our emotions. Those who have known the joy of first fervor know the delight of giving themselves to God in full harmony of mind, will and emotions. But this harmony could not last forever, because God wants to come to us in a deeper manner than can be found by the reasoning mind, the imagination, and the emotions. Also, if the soul must go through the crucifying aridities of the Dark Night, the pleasant emotions shrink back. This is not what they bargained for.

A separation of our faculties of religious experience takes place in regard to the pleasant emotions, and there occurs also a deeper cleavage between the inner soul and the imagination, the memory, and the reasoning intellect. This isolation of the inner soul takes place in the dark contemplation of the Dark Night, and also in the beginnings of clearer contemplation called the prayer of quiet, both of which involve only the inner soul.

This situation is not meant to last forever. When the work of the Dark Night is finished, the interior faculties of reasoning intellect, memory, and imagination have made their surrender to the new mode of reaching God. Then perhaps after not too long a time, there may take place the re-unification of the whole man which was parted in the earlier stage of contemplative prayer. The work of completed purification and the delight of experiencing God by the inner soul eventually allow the separated faculties to gravitate toward giving attention where delight is, and once more to take part in the overflow from the inner enjoyment of God. This is what is meant by the prayer of union. There then is a full union of all the powers of the mind and soul in the enjoyment of the experience of the presence of God. This can come about of course without all this special preparation. God is free and he may give this full prayer before the kind that is only in the inner soul or it may be that the latter, more delicate presence was not recognized earlier.

We can analyze the evolution into the prayer of union from another point of view. Over months or years the soul has been purified of the deep pride that would use God's presence for its self-glorification or self-adulation. The Beloved is now so important, that we want nothing else, neither our own self-centered reflection on the experience, nor any of the things stored up in memory or imagination. Now we are quite completely God's. He may then reward this purification with the power to give ourselves to him in contemplative prayer more completely; all the powers of the mind and will, as well as the emotions, are drawn into the presence, into sharing the wonder that is there within.

The share of these powers and of the emotions is now a subordinate part, whereas in the first fervor it was a predominant one. The soul is now so fixed in God that the emotions do not matter so much; we are content that they are subordinate to the inner experience, not trying blindly to pull the experience of God out to their accustomed mode of feeling, on the surface so to speak. Of course, it is also a delight to have the emotions sharing in the enjoyment of this presence even in this subordinate manner, but it is mostly the freedom and the wholeness in giving ourselves to God that we now appreciate in their regard.

It is not only the pleasant emotions which participate; the less pleasant, even the painful one of fear can also become a companion to some of the prayer of union, and indeed may at times be the principal cause of the immobility of the outward senses in ecstasy. We must not be surprised to find out, after expecting more delight to accompany a greater prayerful closeness to the Beloved, that the prayer of higher contemplation sometimes hurts. This can be so even though we love more than we have before. In fact, love is fighting with the fear, and would endure all the pain if it can only have him whom it so much desires. Even love itself can hurt, in that it wants to break forth against the pressures of the unwilling and immobile body. This condition of painful prayer should eventually change; the sweetness of love will then enfold the soul, and the body feels it too.

We must not forget that there are fluctuations even when this prayer has often or definitively been given. And so we must be careful about desiring more than God wants to give us at the time, careful about trying to go out into the full delight of union, when God can only be found quietly in the inner soul. This is still earth, and the light of glory has not yet been given to strengthen us. The emotions are still capable of becoming exhausted from too much, even of God, unless he chooses to give them special support. Therefore, at times he withdraws the sense of his presence, and we must in patience allow him to do so.

We will not be able to be absorbed in complete recollection at all times, nor even at those times when we are capable of contemplative prayer. Deep recollection may last only a few moments. But it is important that we seize even moments without thinking that they may be only moments. If our giving is to be complete, we must learn not to be mindful of time in any sense, except that which the duties of our state in life and avoidance of undue external singularity may require.

As the prayer has grown more deeply into God, the experience also becomes more than one of simple presence, something which was perhaps too indefinite to be classed in any category that we would normally associate with a person. Now there is more a drawing out, more of an absorption into someone else. There is the definite and strong impression of Another. Being human, the soul wants to delight in the Beloved with all its faculties. In our immediate past, such participation might have meant the temporary termination of contemplative prayer, but now small liberties may be allowed without disturbing the Presence. We are able quietly and briefly to reason, to correct ourselves in prayer, even to tell ourselves that the presence is God, and that those parts of us which are not experiencing this should be at peace about it. Then we can return quietly to the Presence without any diminution of the intensity.

This limited ability is especially helpful when the soul finds itself drawn out or swept out into something without a clear awareness of the Presence. The experience, as we have said, is not always delightful, sometimes it is very painful because we are not yet purified to be sufficiently rid of the fears which inhibit our powers of giving and even our power of looking at him who is drawing us so mightily. Yet we understand that this must be God. No other power, so it seems, would be able to stop us in our operations so completely. But when this presence is less intense and less imperative, we are not so certain. Fortunately the soul has now acquired the limited power to use its reason, as we have just said, and is able to reassure itself that this must be God, and to tell itself and God that it means that its response to this Presence is to be interpreted only as giving itself over to the true but hidden God behind this Power it feels just this much, and then it has peace.

This experience of insecurity, causing the mind to reflect upon itself to see if this is God or if this is prayer, is more often felt in the lower forms of contemplative prayer than in the higher. In the higher forms, the presence of God is more vivid; the mind has no need to reassure itself. But this presence is not so clear in the lower kinds of contemplative prayer, particularly in what is called the prayer of quiet. This indicates a certain purifying quality of the lower forms which does not exist in the higher forms.

In the higher forms the intellect and will are absorbed by the delight of the Beloved. It is true that there may be great purification in the more vivid presence of God, and this is why such prayer is sometimes given to beginners, to withdraw them by delight from sins or from basic attachments. But when the presence is less impelling, less vivid, our imperfections such as insecurity have a chance to intervene. If we want to remain in contact with God, we must learn that giving ourselves does not always mean pouring out ourselves in a torrent of wonder and love, that is, doing something by our own activity, but rather just letting everything else but the intuitive drop away from our consciousness. And then as far as possible, with the spontaneous attention given to the God within, our difficulties may gradually cease.

Rather than to say that the soul will move on schedule out of one kind of prayer into another, never to experience the former kind, a more common evolution is found in the decreasing of difficulties in prayer, principally the disappearance of fearsome self-examination as to the state of prayer. There does come also an increasingly greater facility to respond to him in contemplative prayer, when it is given.

We must not expect that God will share his presence only in rigorous walled-in categories. In the later unitive way it must not surprise us that we may have to seek him in the dark contemplation by the prayer of faith or acquired contemplation (also called the prayer of recollection). Even though infused, clear contemplation is the characteristic often listed for this state, there are times when we will have to use our own efforts to find this much beloved God, not ignoring, surely, a confrontation with the lessons of the life of Christ.

Besides any evolution in contemplative prayer there is the more important evolution in the life of love or in the life of grace. As we grow in love, we see more deeply into the nature and demands of love; in its light we learn its practical consequences in the details of our lives. This evolution evidencing the inner union of grace is a progressive closeness principally observable in the way that God becomes more and more the conscious center of our thoughts and affections. We live for him, not as formerly in the manner of a servant, or even of a close friend whom we are trying to please, but now we are so drawn to him that he is an immediate and all-pervading person upon whom more and more of our conscious life hinges.

The best example we can find of this centeredness upon him is the exclusive and ever deepening love that a man might have for a woman and a woman for a man. In such love, only God knows how many thoughts, movements of the heart, and prayers go out to and for the other . . . or how much is the company, the voice, and the written word longed for, cherished, and recalled . . . or how much does this love become almost the reason and the sustinence for life itself. So in a similar manner does the love of God become the flame which progressively welds together and transforms the scattered motives and movements of each life, not into the temporary and superficial exaltation of first fervor, but perhaps by painful evolution into a God-centered oneness that needs only the full and eternal vision in order to be complete.

Chapter 16

THE DEGREES OF
PRAYERFUL UNION

In this final chapter on prayer, we have the task of distinguishing among the various kinds of prayer which are sometimes associated with the final states of the spiritual life, and of integrating them into the larger, more comprehensive whole of the transforming union as we have seen it in earlier chapters. This task, which may appear formidable, is made simple by keeping in mind two fundamental principles. One is that the basic transforming union between the soul and God consists, not in any form of prayer no matter how exalted, but rather in the degree of sanctifying grace as shown by the heroic degree of the virtues, especially that of love. The other principle, which was to some extent brought out in the last chapter, again is simple, that there is really only one presence of God.

This last statement is true, despite the fact that contemplative prayer, although it usually brings the experience of God simply as God, sometimes brings other manifestations such as an impression of the Blessed Trinity, anyone of the Three Persons, or some attribute of God. These, however, do not affect the diversity of prayer, which is what we are discussing here. Conceivably anyone of these latter could occur in any kind of contemplative prayer. We will apply this second principle by seeing that all of the states of infused prayer can be accounted for, on the one hand, by either the depth of conscious penetration into God or the intensity of God's showing himself, and on the other hand, by the various reactions of soul and body. The degrees of prayer, and even their multitude of names, will thus fall into place intelligibly and according to reality.

We have already said much on the first of these principles. If we are to seek union with God in an essential sense, then the contemplative experiences of betrothal and spiritual marriage are not broad enough, and we again bring St. Teresa of Avila in support of this: "You must not build upon foundations of prayer and contemplation alone, for, unless you strive after the virtues and practice them, you will never grow to be more than dwarfs" (*Interior Castle*, VII, 4).

In practice, the subtle defect in a concentration on the phenomena of the spiritual betrothal or marriage as the final goal of the spiritual life is the same subtle deviation which has often prevented any contemplative prayer: instead of desiring God, and more and more of God, we are in danger of desiring a thing. With the proper distinctions it is, of course, laudable to desire this ultimate conscious oneness with God. But unless great care is taken, our unconscious goal will become personal achievement, rather than oneness with the uncreated God. This deviation is similar to many human marriages in which the bride may think more of her wedding day, and the bridegroom more of his wedding night, than they do about the personal spiritual union with each other.

On the other hand, however, emphasis on the concept of union does not run this danger so much. Union directly implies a correlative, the other, or union with the other. Instead of looking toward some vague, future experience with God, we give him in love the greatest possible oneness we can have in prayer and action here and now, and we are content to live in a union, if he so wills it, that we can comprehend only through faith and hope.

Even if we are given contemplative prayer in any intensity, we can surely be distracted on the way to God by constantly wondering if this or that experience constitutes spiritual betrothal or marriage. In some basic sense we must forget all these things as we reach out for God, or find his presence alive to us. All such speculation can distract from the beauty, the wonder, and the love that he is. Union is best achieved by forgetting about the names and degrees of the prayerful union, and rather thinking principally and somewhat exclusively about the Beloved. It is love that best attracts God to the prayerful union, just as love itself is also the bond of that deeper union which is the likeness to God in sanctifying grace.

In discussing the second point, the unique presence of God, we are dealing with prayerful union, or union experienced in prayer. There is no absolute relationship between the degree of this prayerful union and the degree of essential union of the soul with God. However, enough of those who have become very close to God in this essential union have also had in prayer some intuition of the truth of this union. Surely, it has a rightful place in all discussion of the later spiritual life. There still is, nevertheless, some need for clarification and distinction.

We must avoid making the matter too simple. It would be very easy to say that God's presence is always the same as the degree of sanctifying grace. But this is erroneous, because great graces of prayer are sometimes given to beginners in the spiritual life, and yet a saint may enjoy only the dimmest of contemplative prayer, if that. Likewise it would be too simple to say that God's presence is constant within us, and that we receive an intuition of it according to our degree of purification. Obviously the same two reasons just given are applicable here also. Therefore, we hold a twofold conclusion: first, that God does at times manifest his presence, the one presence, in different degrees, and then also, that there is a diverse and varying ability or facility on our part to respond to it.

To say that there is a relative ability or facility in contemplative prayer, does not conflict with the fact that all such prayer is given or infused. For example, a physical condition such as illness or a psychological condition brought about by an overly emotional experience, or even the pressures of duty, can dim or temporarily obliterate this facility to sense the presence of God.

The observation that greater purification is required for greater union in prayer is not without truth in practice, provided that we understand it to be true only in general. Although we do not now conduct any great campaigns to detach ourselves from creatures, this does not mean that there is no further detachment. God will work out our further purification by his inner enlightenment or by providential changes of circumstances. He will still use our mistakes to teach us.

Although we cannot conclude, here or elsewhere, that in every aridity God is now teaching us a specific lesson about inordinate attachment to creatures, and that therefore, we must search out the person or thing from which we are to be detached, still there are times when cause and effect are sufficiently evident. We will see him withdraw the sense of his presence when we have imprudently turned toward creatures, as with St. Catherine of Siena when she was deliberately, though partially, distracted in prayer. Our closeness to God in prayer can, within obvious limits, now itself become a teacher, not a teacher that rules by anxiety, but one which will make us watchful for our weaknesses.

In our efforts toward clarification, we are confronted with a confusing number of kinds of experience along with their various names. Viewing these as the qualifications necessary to be in the unitive way, we can understand why many people have eliminated themselves after a discouraged look. But if we understand that there are only three basic ways in which God's presence is with us in contemplative prayer, the situation becomes simple of comprehension and seems not impossible of attainment. The same God is present in all three, God as God in the simplicity of his nature, although it matters little for our purposes here if there is any emphasis on a particular attribute or an impression of a Divine Person. Thus we distinguish first the presence of God which is given but not ordinarily felt, the dark contemplation of the Dark Night. Then we can distinguish two basic kinds of clearer contemplative prayer.

We have already discussed the two kinds of clear contemplation, the one usually called the prayer of quiet, which affects only the intuitive intellect and the will, and the other, the prayer of union, in which the presence is stronger, strong enough to capture our whole intellectual, volitional, and emotional structure. Between these two there are varying degrees. But if we look to the states of prayer which are listed as being beyond the prayer of union, we will expect somehow a totally different kind of presence of God, and so consequently, a different kind of prayer. The truth is, that they are only intensifications of the same simple presence which causes all contemplative prayer. The distinguishing differences from the prayer of union, other than this intensification, are mostly on the part of ourselves.

This simplification is not an oversimplification, because we shall not attempt to suppress the principal names of the kinds of prayer which are listed after the prayer of union. What we are proposing in this simplification is to explain these latter kinds of prayer in an analytical fashion, which will make them less mysterious and much more easily understood.

The word "union" in the prayer of union does not refer specifically to conscious union with God, since the prayer of quiet is also a conscious union, although not so strongly unmistakable. Rather it refers to the union of intellect, will, internal senses, and emotions in one simple experience. Furthermore, on the part of God there is no essential difference between the prayer of union and ecstatic or rapturous prayer, except that the presence of God may be stronger. This simple prayer of union we differentiate into ecstasy and its similar forms, not by any essential internal causes or effects, but only by the external physical effects which an intenser form of this prayer may cause in certain people.

Thus, since all contemplative prayer has degrees, there may come times when the prayer of union becomes so strong or intense, that the body is no longer able to sustain itself outwardly. Indeed, the capture of all the internal senses (which are physical in nature) by the prayer of union, more easily brings it into contact with the psychological areas which, materially speaking, produce the unconsciousness. The resulting external unconsciousness is in general called ecstasy or rapture, depending on whether the strong presence of God and the unconsciousness come gradually or suddenly. Thus in their bare essentials these two mysterious states of prayer become quite simple. All the other externally unconscious states of prayer are merely variations of these.

There is the kind of prayer called ecstasy. There is nothing very mysterious about it in principle, although we can make it too simple by seeing nothing more in it than the mere mental abstraction found in an absent-minded professor. It is a going out of oneself, so to speak, because of the vivid and attractive presence of God. St. Teresa of Avila, who was familiar with it, describes the physical aspects of it (See *Life*, ch. 18 and 20). She tells us that it can be felt coming on gradually and gently as the perception of the presence of God becomes more difficult to bear. The body temperature falls, the breathing slows, and the general physical result is immobility and rigidity.

There are degrees of this absorption. The relatively short time of deepest absorption is followed by a gradual return to external reality through what can be called the prayer of quiet, which may last for hours or even days. The experience can be delightful or painful, but even the pain is embraced.

The difference between this and the simple prayer of union is that, the internal senses are held in the wonder of God, and now the external senses no longer function either. If it be objected that this state is no different from that of a trance or fainting spell, it must be affirmed that the person in ecstasy is unconscious only to what is going on outside of him. Unlike the person in a faint, he is intensely alive to the presence of God within.

Love is the cause of this fixation, and perhaps in some cases and to a lesser degree it is also fear. In the mental fixation itself, it is not unlike the concentration of the scholar or the reader of an interesting book, except that it is much more deeply rooted and intense. As St. Thomas says when speaking on ecstasy, "To intently dwell on one thing draws the mind from other things" (I, II; 28;3). Here we are in such vivid contact with God that the mind and will go out to him or are drawn out to him with such intensity that some of the natural processes are changed or interrupted. This must not therefore, be thought miraculous, nor that God bestows ecstasy as a gift. What he does is to show himself more clearly and the soul does the rest, leaving the body inert, primarily because of the weakness of the psychological powers of the body.

It will help to understand ecstasy if we consider it as a weakness. St. Teresa calls it an infirmity (See *Interior Castle*, VII, 3). Some of the saints have had extraordinarily vivid experiences of God, and yet never had an ecstasy. The state that is called spiritual marriage, considered as a state of prayer, is characterized by the close presence and love of God, but without this "troublesome" experience (St. Teresa's word for it). The faculties hitherto caught up or paralyzed by the experience have become accustomed to the marvel of God's closeness. This happens either by God's action directly, or better, by grace and nature combined.

Ecstasy can also be characterized as a way in which God can get our undivided attention. From this point of view it may indeed be brought on occasionally even in those who have now gone beyond this state of prayer, as it did to Peter in Joppa (Ac 10:10). The attention is so undivided that the soul can become unaware even of the self, except in its center core and then only as it is related to great feelings of love for God. The soul can thus say as did St. Paul in a similar context: "Whether in the body or out of the body, I do not know, God knows" (2 Cor 12:2).

A few more varieties of this kind of prayer are usually distinguished. The first is rapture. This primarily concerns the manner in which God approaches. He may come in such a manner that there is a certain violence in going out of oneself, whereas ordinary ecstasy can be felt gradually coming on. This violence can be the result of a combination of God's sudden and intense approach together with the intensity of our love in responding to him. In other respects it does not differ from ecstasy. Indeed St. Teresa uses the terms almost interchangeably: "I should like, with the help of God, to be able to describe the difference between union and rapture, or elevation, or what they call flight of the spirit, or transport—it is all one. I mean that these different names all refer to the same thing, which is also called ecstasy" (*Life*, ch. 20). However, she does also use rapture in the restricted sense (e.g. *Interior Castle*, VI, 5, or St. Thomas, II,II;175; 1 and 2).

It is principally in the case of rapture that we come upon the experience of painful contemplative prayer. Pain can at times also be felt in all the less intense forms of infused prayer, including the dark contemplation. The reasons are in general obvious: the unfamiliarity of the soul with what is happening, an unconscious fear because of its own uncleanness before God, and stubborn psychological barriers such as a resistance to being loved for one's own sake. All these may intrude themselves into ecstasy and rapture, but in addition there is now the greater manifestation of (or penetration into) the uncreated magnificence that is God, as well as the new fear of being seen in this unconscious state by others.

St. Francis de Sales gives another cause of pain, which in one way or another can also be experienced at lower levels of prayer. Here, however, since the presence of God is stronger and thus can be more alluring, the pain can be especially great. "He (God) gives the soul admirable sentiments of and incomparable attractions for his sovereign goodness, as if pressing it and soliciting it to love him. . . . It feels a pain which can have no equal. At the same time that it is powerfully drawn to fly toward its dear well-beloved, it is also kept back and cannot fly, being chained to the base miseries of this mortal life and of the soul's powerlessness" (*Treatise on the Love of God*, bk, VI, ch. 13. See also St. Teresa, *Life*, ch. 20).

In rapture, however, there is added to all these causes of pain the suddenness and the strength of the Lord's coming, which understandably increase the fear, the pain, and perhaps also the love.

In summary, the crucial element causing pain in contemplative prayer is basically the stress between the presence of God, even when dimly felt, and the ability of the human psyche and physical organism to bear it. Thus, those who are in a less intense form of this prayer, and who are at present unable to bear much of the presence of God without flinching from it, may indeed experience some pain. But their pain is in no way to be compared with that sometimes felt by those who are given a more intense impression of this union. How well it is said that even the perfectly purified souls in heaven would be unable to endure the beatific vision if they were not supported by a special strengthening called the light of glory (*lumen gloriae*) (See Denz-Banw. no. 475; also St. Thomas I;12;5).

The pain is physical as well as spiritual and psychological. St. John of the Cross is perhaps describing extreme cases: "For at times the torture felt in such visits of rapture is so great that there is no torture which so wrenches asunder the bones and straitens the physical nature—so much so that unless God provided for the soul, its life would come to an end" (*Spiritual Canticle*, st. 13).

Thus, it can easily be seen that although the favor of God is greater in higher prayer, trials of all kinds still may be frequent. Much courage, therefore, is needed as well as love. The false picture of ecstasy and rapture as a refuge of the weak and of those seeking mere escape is refuted by the hard facts of the spiritual life from its beginnings to its culmination. Courage enables us to bear these sufferings but love makes us embrace them. And we would suffer these and more, rather than to lose God, or even this contact with God or the hope of greater contact with him.

The response to God in rapture, though immediate and vehement in this crucifixion of love and suffering, is none the less freely given. We respond to God by an instinct of love freely, as for example, married partners may respond to married love passionately, yet freely. Here in ecstasy and rapture our response is free, not only by our general intention to give ourselves to God as completely as we can, but also by our very nature itself which is so created as to find its supreme fulfillment only in God. Yet in this outpouring of our nature into God our freedom comes close to being rather a movement of necessity. When God is thus seen sufficiently and clearly (as indeed he will be perfectly clear to us in the beatific vision) our will cannot, or can hardly, refuse to go out to him in rapture or in higher prayer, since it was made to respond to this total and perfect Good (St. Thomas, I;82;2).

Those who are subject to this state of ecstasy are usually obliged to conduct their affairs in an orderly manner, and this leaves only a limited time for full abandonment to the drawing or demanding presence within. Thus, they must adopt in one way or another, and insofar as it is possible, some means of legitimately distracting themselves from this attraction. This is not a rejection of God or a wasting of his gifts; rather it is an acceptance of his full will, a will which at times requires this resistance because of other duties of justice of charity to others or even to oneself—even as the cares of married life often require resistance to loving between spouses.

This distraction can be done in various ways. One of the more simple is to limit the time given to prayer on any one occasion. One teaching Sister could not allow herself more than a limited time before the Blessed Sacrament or she would not have been able to leave.

Another means which has proved somewhat successful is to take deep breaths when one senses the ecstasy is coming on. It is noticeable during ecstasy that breathing diminishes radically and in some cases almost stops completely. This is probably a reason for the drop in bodily temperature mentioned by St. Teresa. Deep breathing may somehow keep the bodily processes working more efficiently and so immobility is less likely to take place. Attention to the breathing, while it may not distract from God's presence entirely, gives the mind an anchor in its own psyche for, once deeply into ecstasy, one is for all practical purposes outside the body.

There is also a varying ability to distract the mind from the drawing toward the presence within. We are told that St. John of the Cross would rub his knuckles against the wall of the cloister and fix his attention on that. Any other kind of physical pressure or motion may be sufficient, even that of a finger or the hand. Or the mind may be able simply to concentrate, as did that of St. Thomas Aquinas, who seems to have concentrated as he willed, and so ecstasy did not interfere with his life of intense work in the midst of an intense life of prayer.

One is apt to concede this ability to men more than to women since woman's nature impels them more wholeheartedly toward whatever they are doing, especially as to loving. But men have not been entirely successful in this by any means. St. Philip Neri was unable to stop ecstasies at Mass for years, much though he tried to keep from exhausting his servers. Even St. Thomas in the last three months of his life either found the inner light now shining more brightly, or perhaps had exhausted his robust physique by the amazing literary output of his last five years and now found himself too weak to resist the light. Or it may be that, since he realized interiorly that his work was now over, even though unfinished, there was no longer the need to exercise the great concentration away from total communion with God. Perhaps even St. Paul had this problem of distracting himself from God. This text has been variously interpreted but it may bear this interpretation too: "For if we are beside ourselves, it is for God; if we are in our right mind, it is for you. For the love of Christ controls us" (2 Cor 5:13, 14).

Attempts to distract are, therefore, not always successful but more can be done than one thinks at the time—certainly more can be done than one feels inclined to do at the time. Thus, the presence of God in this period can mean a discipline, and even a cross. This is God's loving providence, because an obvious temptation here is to vanity and pride—obvious objectively but probably only subtly perceptible to the person involved. Much prayer for humility must accompany all graces of prayer, even these.

Besides ecstasy and rapture, another variety of this kind of prayer, flight of the spirit, is often mentioned. We have already seen that St. Teresa considers this to be the same as rapture or ecstasy, but St. John of the Cross seems to give it the particular quality of knowledge of God in prayer, but stresses that it is "the love which comes from this knowledge" (*Spiritual Canticle*, st. 13). If on the other hand it is specific knowledge of God or his mysteries, it would seem to be an extraordinary grace, a *gratia gratis data*, which is not in the ordinary unitive way we have been considering. By knowledge here we must understand the knowledge proper to contemplative prayer, a knowledge which is often indistinct even when powerfully unmistakable in its ability to draw us.

This predominance of the intellect in this form of contemplative prayer is not entirely new at this stage of development. From the very beginnings of the consciousness of God's infused presence it is sometimes the will rather than the intellect that is more absorbed. In intellectual love, sometimes it is more the intellect in a loving awe and wonder, and still at other times the prayer comes and goes without either faculty being in noticeable predominance. It would be a mistake to try to find out.

A particularly deep and strong form of the prayer of union is called divine touches, using the word "touch" as giving a stronger impression of closeness or union than that of sight ("contemplation"), which is the more usual metaphor to describe infused prayer. Neither "contemplation" nor "touches" has anything to do with visions or actual touches (See *Living Flame of Love*, St. II, 22).

If we searched, we would come upon other names for other experiences of the prayer of union, but names should never become major guideposts. Even for those in this state the detailed knowledge of the varieties is unnecessary, except possibly and occasionally for reassurance for them or for their directors. For those not in this state or concerned with direction, too much knowledge may be harmful, both because of the danger inherent in watching themselves too closely, and because of the blindness caused by the expectation of these things, a blindness to the more important and essential union of God through love and the other virtues. If we are looking for union with God in prayer, then we must accept whatever prayer he gives at at the moment. Contemplative prayer can be an enormous help toward essential union in grace, since it gives some glimmer of what he is like.

Therefore, we can see that there is no essential difference on the part of the presence of God in all these states which are, as we have said, essentially the prayer of union, the prayer in which the presence is strong and unmistakable. The difference arises from the intensity of the presence on the part of God and from the various reactions, spiritual, psychological, and physical, on the part of the person. The action is not extraordinary on the part of God, as it would be if this were a vision or a revelation, but the reaction is out of the ordinary on our part in the case of ecstasy and rapture, because of weakness as we have said.

By means of these two ideas ecstasy and rapture lose some of their mysteriousness. From these ideas, as well as from authentic personal descriptions such as those of St. Teresa, we can also see what ecstasy and rapture are not. Against those who confuse the simple truth by trying to identify these spiritual states with other phenomena, the dissimilarities can be important.

We have already mentioned the attempt to reduce ecstasy to a mere fainting spell, and that this is disproved by the fact that the mind is not unconscious within, but on the contrary is very alive in the delight of the presence of God which drew it so irresistibly. Another difference is that, whereas in a faint the body is limp, in ecstasy and rapture "the body normally remains as if dead and unable of itself to do anything: it continues in the same state as it was when the rapture came upon it—in a sitting position, for example, or with the hands open or shut" (*Life*, ch. 20). "It cannot even move its hand without great pain; its eyes involuntarily close, or, if they remain open, they can hardly see" (*ib.* ch. 18).

The person in a faint has no recollection of anything going on in his mind, but the mind in simple ecstasy or rapture remembers well that it was "rejoicing in some good thing in which are comprised all good things at once" (*ib.*). And in those cases of ecstasy or rapture which involve some revelation, "after coming to itself, the souls will remember that revelation of the great things that it has seen" (*Interior Castle*, VI, 4).

From the above it can also easily be seen that ecstasy and rapture are not physical paroxisms, such as an epileptic seizure, where there is no consciousness of memory. "It is not like a swoon or paroxism so that it can understand nothing either within itself or without" (*ib.*). The mind and will are alive in God while the external senses are lifeless. "This lasts only for a short time. . . . The body seems to come partly to itself again. . . . Complete ecstasy, therefore, does not last very long" (*ib.*, *Life*, ch. 16 and 19; *Foundations*, ch. 6).

Nor are these spiritual states some form of somnambulism. In the latter some remarkable things are possible, such as walking in sleep on high, dangerous places, writing letters, or solving mathematical problems that one would be unable to do when awake. But there is no memory of having done so. In ordinary ecstasy or rapture the person does not move, and he has a vivid memory of the internal experience. A more obvious difference is that these mystical experiences are simply not sleep experiences. The soul can be absorbed into the vivid presence of God in any occupation, even outside of prayer. This is especially true of rapture.

Similar to somnambulism is the deep trance of those under complete hypnosis, and this similarity with ecstasy and rapture is sometimes offered to explain these mystical phenomena. But after we allow for this similarity, there is little else to indicate a similar source. Like much of the other completely natural explanations, the person under a complete trance typically will not remember what happened (unless told to do so by the hypnotist). Oppositely, the person in ecstasy or rapture will remember the internal experience. Although he will not be able to recreate the sublimity of it at will, he still has a deep impression of what it was.

This inability to recreate voluntarily the internal experience also constitutes a real difference from the state of hypnosis, which is entered by a definite, repeatable technique involving real or imaginary objects. But ecstasy and rapture cannot be repeated at will but must wait for the divine motion on the waters of the soul. Likewise, concrete objects or images used by the hypnotist also differentiate it from the mystical experiences, which are intellectual in their fundamental nature, even though not with the absolute intellectual clarity of the beatific vision.

There is a further dissimilarity even in the rigidity of the body. The hypnotic subject will move readily at the command of the hypnotist, whereas St. Teresa of Avila tells us that in these mystical states the body can hardly move even partially, and then only with great pain.

In hypnosis the subject is gradually moved into a deeper and deeper trance, and this may seem to indicate a similarity with simple ecstasy described above. This similarity would seem to indicate self-hypnosis on the part of the mystic.

To clarify this we must first of all admit that we do not adequately know the physiological and psychological or clinical reasons for the unconscious state or trance of the mystic in ecstasy or rapture, and the same can be said of hypnosis and even of the simple daily experience of sleep. A similar effect, however, can easily have a different cause. A headache may come from any number of causes, physical or emotional. We must therefore, investigate the cause of the experience as well as those effects which we can reach.

In the case of simple ecstasy the person enters into it through what seems to be the prayer of quiet becoming deeper, into the prayer of union. Then at some time the psychological and physical apparatus becomes unhinged and the mind becomes unconscious to all except the loving presence of God enjoyed within, and the body assumes a trancelike state. This would seem to indicate the gradual process of hypnotism to a deeper and deeper level.

There is nothing in the simple presence of God (as such) which produces ecstasy because, as St. Teresa tells us, one is able to live in this simple presence of God for days with no onset of a trance. Likewise in the more perfect prayer of the transforming union, beyond ecstasy, the person lives in the strong presence of God without going into ecstasy.

In these two experiences of states of prayer, both lower and higher than ecstasy, we have clear evidence of some other cause than the narrowing of the field of consciousness which somewhat describes the absorption into hypnosis. The cause therefore, of ecstasy is not the oneness of concentration of the hypnotic subject. It is the response of the weak psychological and physical powers of the human nature involved in this particular experience of the awesomeness or impelling goodness of God.

This conclusion is supported by the experience of rapture. As a state of prayer it differs from ecstasy only in the strong, sudden movement by God which brings it on. Here we do not have the slow process of ecstasy but rather a sudden shock, so to speak, which carries the mind and will away from certain normal physical and psychological operations, irresistibly and without warning. The whole experience is there all at once, not a way to describe self-hypnosis, but rather indicates that something has come from outside the psyche, as those reliable persons who experience it tell us that it does. For it is not a voluntary experience as self-hypnosis would be, but "very often I should be glad to resist, and I exert all my strength to do so, in particular at times when it happens in public. . . . Occasionally I have been able to make some resistance, but at the cost of great exhaustion. . . . At other times, resistance has been impossible" (*Life*, ch. 20).

One of the most feeble attempts to explain away ecstasy and rapture is to equate them with sexual orgasm, which often implies being carried out of oneself. This explanation assumes, however, that people like St. Teresa and St. John of the Cross were so totally ignorant of sexual passion that they were self-deluded into thinking that what is an easily recognized organic experience, was on the contrary some sublime, spiritual (that is, non-material) flight. The sober truth is that we must accept as a fact the ability to recognize sexual feelings by some (at least) who have experienced higher mystical prayer. For instance St. Teresa's frequent assertions that in her earlier life she had been a great sinner are to be taken quite literally. Besides, when she describes ecstasy or rapture, not only is she not describing orgasm, but clearly is describing something else: "This pleasure is greater than any worldly pleasure" (*Foundations*, ch. 6).

As for St. John of the Cross, he openly confronts the problem of the involvement of sexual passion in prayer. He identifies it, not as a cause of religious experience, but as a result of overly emotional religious experience. Furthermore, he finds that it is a problem when the emotions are still active and not under control in certain people in the *earlier* stages of the spiritual life (*Dark Night*, bk. I, ch. 4 and 13).

Marital love may indeed at times give feelings which are rightly termed sublime, but this is not a reason for narrowing all sublime experience to the sexual and declaring that spiritual ecstasy must be sexual because it too is sublime. How different from this human ecstasy, brought about by powerful emotions and the excitation of the sexually sensitive areas of the body, is the spiritual ecstasy in which the soul "lets itself pass and flow into what it loves; it does not spring out of itself by a sudden leap, nor does it cling as by a joining or union, but it gently glides as a fluid and liquid thing, into the divinity whom it loves" (St. Francis de Sales, *Treatise on the Love of God*, VI, 12). Ecstasy and rapture are brought about by an intellectual awareness and not by emotional arousal.

How can an experience be logically called sexual when there is no such excitation? In sexual orgasm the body has its own total way of reacting. This is clearly not the physical reaction of ecstasy and rapture. Moreover, the mind is clear in these mystical states,

even though absorbed in love, something not true in the fulfillment of sexual passion. If it be the kind of ecstasy or rapture in
which messages are given, these are transmitted either at the time
or on coming out of the ecstasy—something not experienced in
orgasm.

Along with establishing ecstasy and rapture as interdependent
spiritual, psychological, and physical phenomena in their own
right, we do not deny the existence of quasi-religious experiences
somewhat similar in various aspects. Two of these are the trance
of the medium in spiritualism and the pseudo-ecstasies or trances
of hysterical or highly emotional persons. The fact that these exist
does not detract from the fact of mystical ecstasy, although attempts are made to put all of them in the same loose category.

A trancelike rigidity can be experienced by spiritualist
mediums and yet, even when there is no reason to suspect
trickery, the important fact is that the medium is in a trance and
not in ecstasy. An alleged spirit takes over the body of the medium
for the purpose of communication. Contrary to ecstasy, the soul is
not drawn out of the normal operations of its physical and
psychological powers by a compelling absorption into God.

Another indication of the great difference between ecstasy
and such a trance is the type of communication given. The words
reported by the medium have nothing of the sublime. On the
contrary, they are commonplace utterances which the medium
may not remember afterwards. Often enough they have been of
an order as to suggest to some investigators the presence of the
evil spirit. These results are essentially different from the communications of those in ecstasies or raptures in which revelations
or visions are transmitted, as for instance, with St. Catherine of
Siena, an unlearned daughter of a wool-dyer, whose *Dialogue*
dictated in ecstasy is one of the spiritual masterpieces of the
Christian world.

Less surprising are the attempts to assign the cause of ecstasy
and rapture to hysteria. This is less surprising because it has a
certain limited validity which tends to make the whole, sweeping
but erroneous conclusion plausible. The Church has had enough
experience with sincere, but false mystics to understand the argu-

ment and to accept hysteria, not as an explanation of all higher
mystical phenomena, but as a test which all true mystical experience must pass.

Hysteria, or whatever clinical name may be used, is a nervous
and psychological disorder which can easily bring on delusions.
These delusions can be of any kind, and they can be religious. Like
all such disorders it shows characteristic evidence of itself, and this
may be summarized as a serious lack of mental and emotional
balance. The subject is led more by emotional than by rational
stimuli. There is no whole personality and therefore, the subject
of alleged religious experiences will not have all the virtues in a
high degree, but may rather have a concentration on those which
tend toward display or which bring attention to oneself in the
milieu where approval or distinction is desired, at least unconsciously. Thus, it needs to be shown that the true mystic has
spiritual and human qualities of a high order and can exercise
responsible conduct, especially under extreme difficulties.

This does not mean that God cannot bend down even further
than usual and grant graces of prayer to the most unfitted of us.
But the truth will be shown in the effects which will be good, even
though short of high perfection, even perhaps such as will enable
this kind of person merely to survive, by the comfort or consolation given by God in the experience. Yet without balance of mind,
character, and emotions such experiences remain suspect. Therefore any such account of higher prayer or extraordinary communications or visions should be considered at best as personal
graces not to be divulged in general to others because of the great
danger of illusion present or almost sure to come because of the
demands or, oppositely, the ridicule of others.

Even in view of this possibility of deception, only one not
familiar with the literature of Catholic mysticism could grasp at
hysteria as a universal explanation for phenomena they do not
want to accept either because they do not accept the reality of
God, or because they do not think God would love so intimately or
familiarly. It is not as if the mystics themselves were all in ignor-
ance of the possibility of self-deceptive religious experience or

were not anxious to combat such deception, whether well-intentioned or not. St. Teresa's agonies of doubt caused by the doubts of others are a matter of record (See *Life*, ch. 23). Much later as a mystic who had survived investigation by the Spanish Inquisition she frequently warns her sisters about the exaggeration which can come to religious of a melancholic temperament. Specifically she wrote at great length on this subject of illusion to the superiors under her jurisdiction (See *Foundations*, ch. 6).

St. Teresa's estimate of herself is far different from what is a hysterical subject. Using the word "emotional" in a derogatory sense, she says "I am not in the least emotional; on the contrary my hardness of heart sometimes worries me" (*Interior Castle*, VI, 6). One of the differences between true mystical experiences and the mental condition of hysterical people is that simple ecstasy and rapture are caused by an intellectual perception—indeed since mystical prayer intuitively reaches out to God, it is the highest activity of the human intellect—whereas the phenomena of the hysterical persons principally is emotional and comes largely from phantasms in the imagination.

For instance, far from being the writings of a deranged or overwrought woman, anyone who doubts St. Teresa is invited to read her *Life*, written by herself, in order to discover the ingenuousness and balance of her personality. Indeed her writings (as well as those of St. John of the Cross) occupy an acknowledged eminence in the literature of the world. Besides, these two people accomplished much in the practical world. St. John of the Cross was entrusted with high administrative offices in his religious order, and the accomplishments of St. Teresa in founding her seventeen convents, most of them without any financial or influential help in the beginning (and often with much opposition) argues for a high level of human qualities, not to speak of the divine. Such responsibilities and accomplishments indicate anything but a disordered mental state. Likewise, if we were to compile even a short list of the great women of Western civilization, we would surely have to include St. Teresa, and also St. Catherine of Siena as well both of whom have been declared Doctors of the

Church, after vigorous investigation, an honor shared by only a very small number of men, St. Augustine and St. Thomas Aquinas, for instance.

Allowing for some understandable, adverse physical effects, as we have indicated earlier, we can even offer good physical effects arising from ordinary ecstasy as a strong indication of the absence of a diseased psyche. Again St. Teresa is our witness: "This prayer, for however long it may last, does no harm; at least it has never done any for me, nor do I ever remember feeling any ill effects after the Lord has granted me this favor, however unwell I may have been; indeed I am generally much the better for it" (*Life*, ch. 18).

St. John of the Cross agrees, although he is speaking principally of the prayer of the transforming union itself: "And in this good which comes to the soul the unction of the Holy Spirit sometimes overflows into the body, and this is enjoyed by all the substance of sense and all the members of the body and the very marrow and bones, not feebly as is usually the case, but with a feeling of great delight and glory, which is felt even in the remotest joints of the feet and hands. And the body feels such glory in the glory of the soul that it magnifies God after its own manner, perceiving that he is in its very bones, even as David said, 'All my bones shall say, "God, who is like unto Thee?" ' And since all that can be said of such matters is less than the truth, it suffices to say of the bodily experience, as of the spiritual, that it savors of eternal life" (*Living Flame*, st. 2, no. 22).

These physical effects, though valuable, are not as strong or coercive a criterion of true ecstasy as the moral and spiritual effects. Our Lord insists, "By their fruits you shall know them" (Mt 7:16). True mystical experiences will in general result in advances in the life of the virtues, such as humility and submission to the will of God, and in concern for our neighbor (e.g., St. Teresa, *Life*, ch. 19, 20, 21). One cannot honestly expect that the good spiritual and moral effects and the outstanding natural qualities, such as strength of will and sharp intellect, such as have occurred in so many of the saints who knew mystical experience, can come from a life based on unreality. Effects do not rise above their causes.

It is especially through these good spiritual and moral effects that we are principally able to distinguish between ecstasies and raptures which result from contact with God and those that proceed from an evil spirit. Indeed much of the original opposition to St. Teresa was occasioned by the unmasking of a false mystic who confessed to great voluntary deceptions by the devil. St. Teresa had to make her way against the current of her immediate times. But God who was leading her, was able to show by her personal life the truth that it was his hand that was leading her.

Like all contemplative prayer no one will seek to be absorbed into ecstasy or rapture. Indeed one way to prevent true ecstasy would be to seek it. The degree of prayerful union intense enough to bring absorption must come from God, and absorption comes (if it comes) by seeking God. "The venerable and blessed father Fray John of the Cross was once asked how a man went into ecstasy. 'By renouncing his own will,' he replied, 'and doing the will of God' " (*Points of Love*, no. 65).

St. Francis de Sales brings such vain ambitions down to earth: "Blessed are they who live a superhuman and ecstatic life raised above themselves (that is, overcoming themselves and their natural inclinations), though they may not be raised above themselves in prayer. There are many saints in heaven who were never in ecstasy or rapture of contemplation. For, how many martyrs and great saints do we see in history never to have had any other privilege in prayer than that of devotion or fervor" (*Treatise on the Love of God*, bk. 7, ch. 7).

Having distinguished ecstasy from other phenomena which, though similar, are not the same, and also having given some criteria to identify true ecstasy, we will now attempt to indicate how a person may be drawn into what is thought to be ecstasy but is not. We leave out pathological cases which are due to psychological and nervous disorders, and suggest two ways that this could happen to someone who is normal in the accepted sense of the word. One way is self-induced and the other is the initiative of the devil.

The first way is by exaggeration of a natural reaction. We all tend to turn our minds away from unpleasant situations—or should do so rather than to brood over them. Nature itself tends to block out certain unpleasant and unsupportable situations, for instance, in extreme cases by mental shock. Thus in the face of a prolonged, unpleasant situation a person gifted with a lower form of prayer, contemplative or not, will tend to turn inwards to God in order to obtain relief. As such this is a normal response, comparable to the many natural ways that bring about the same effect, such as doing some agreeable work requiring close attention or reading an interesting book. In some people with or without experience in prayer the flight from the unpleasant situation may be more total and can result in the temporary oblivion characteristic of true ecstasy.

The experience of false ecstasy is due essentially to our response and not to the intensity of what is given by God. An example from a similar situation may help to understand this. A priest or other counselor must be careful in his speech with women whom he is helping in difficulties, especially involving loneliness and frustration. An unguarded, overly sympathetic or tender word may bring on a highly emotional response, like a spark igniting dry grass. Similarly the same effect can follow in the life of prayer: a small grace of prayer can be unconsciously enlarged so as to be thought a great one. Souls in loneliness or other oppressive states of the psyche can grasp this consolation and use it as a heavy weight to sink into themselves, with the emotions supplying for the sweetness of true ecstasy. This is all the more likely to happen when there is still much residual pride in the soul, unnoticed by the person himself.

This concurrence with pride is all the more likely when the ecstasy is not self-induced, consciously or unconsciously, but induced by the devil. A study of satanism shows that he can produce a facsimile of what is from God. Even some of the saints have, at times in their lives, had to admit that what they thought was divine consolation was from the opposite source. A humble, well-balanced, and experienced person may catch the counterfeit quickly enough, but a mind prepared to accept anything that promises the extraordinary, or one whose psyche demands relief, can fall under this clever diabolic influence (even though not wanting to have anything to do with the devil) and can experience in prayer what they sincerely believe is from God. This shows the need for prudent help from a director or confessor, and it may even take a relatively long time even for these to make a final judgment.

It goes without saying that these two sources of illusion can be working at the same time, for the devil does not usually prey on our strengths but uses our weaknesses against us.

Both of these ways to mistaken ecstasy can be detected in the persistent failure to grow in the ordinary, hidden virtues, despite a pious demeanor and reputation.

The definite experience of a spiritual betrothal, which is often associated with ecstasy or rapture, has no essential place on our spiritual journey. The same is true of a definite spiritual marriage, which is often confused with the final state of contemplative prayer of union which we are now to discuss. Indeed this final state of prayer is often named the spiritual marriage. But in truth neither the implied experience of some kind of marriage nor the prayer as we will outline it are essential to the union of the soul and God in the highest degrees of sanctifying grace offered to men, and shown by the heroic degree of the virtues.

It may appear that our emphasis on what is essential to the transforming union is a minimizing of the value and privilege of the mystical experiences of spiritual betrothal and marriage. In attempting to reach a balance, we may have pushed too hard. This is certainly not our intention. Indeed if such experiences are given, they are to be considered enormous graces, to be carefully lived up to, and to be safeguarded by much prayer for fidelity, just as would be the case in human betrothal and marriage.

As guideposts they are unreliable because they may never occur. Too great a dependence on the two terms may tend to categorize the spiritual life, which often is an imperceptible flow from one state to another. St. Teresa of Avila gives us confirmation precisely at this juncture. In going from the consideration of prayerful ecstasy, sometimes exemplified by spiritual betrothal, to the state of spiritual marriage, we pass from her Sixth to her Seventh Mansion. Instead of a definite gap between the two, she specifically indicates that these "might be fused into one: there is no closed door to separate the one from the other" (*Interior Castle*, VI, 6).

If we look upon the ecstatic states primarily as a response of human weakness to the surpassing love and wonder of God, we will not be surprised that the final state of the prayer of union, often called spiritual marriage, is in general one of tranquility. The senses, both internal and external, have now been given the power to operate at the same time that God is intensely loved and enjoyed within, as we have seen from the description by St. John of the Cross just given. The whole man has been strengthened and is wholly under the influence of God while acting from the communion which comes from this presence. Although ecstasies and raptures are apt to be rare, perhaps to cease altogether, the mind and will are given over to God when in prayer, in immeasurable depth and delight. Outside of prayer, the will is held by the presence of God and yet we will be able to conduct the ordinary affairs of life.

This is indeed an advance toward our state in heaven when our love of God will be much more intense, and yet will allow our human faculties of sight, hearing, and touch, as well as our reason, their full operation.

This freeing of the faculties to operate is not without a deep significance for our attitude toward this final state of prayer. Although during the time set aside for love there is an exclusiveness surrounding the soul and God, just as in marriage, it would not be true to generalize this exclusiveness into the totality of life. The time we are with God in prayer, cannot be the norm for all the hours of the day. We are normally obliged, even in this state of conscious union, to have other people and other things in our lives. Toward these we will have obligations in justice and in charity.

Even though the word "marriage" has been the source of much confusion in the spiritual life, here in this intense, conscious, prayerful union, it can be a legitimate simile. Just as in marriage the deeper love of God, at times perhaps difficult to control earlier and interfering with normal duties, now becomes a tranquil but intimate, ever-deepening relationship. As in ideal marriage, this love is at the heart of the oneness, and in that sense is almost the whole of it. Love is the relatively constant experience, and it is the motive for all else. Love is given and received, as in marriage, because of the other; love itself is the reward for everything. The mind and will are given to this love without any self-conscious reflection, and without any wish except to be with the Beloved and to accomplish his will.

No attempt is being made here to describe this love from the inside, so to speak, since it would be as futile as trying to tell children (were that lawful or prudent) what love the man and wife experience in their intimacy. It is enough to say that God is undeniably present as he never was before, and that the soul responds. Somehow an ultimate seems to have been reached, especially in tranquility of full possession. To one who has this embrace of God, no more will need to be said, nor can be said.

Despite the beauty and congruity of the term "spiritual marriage" for this prayer, however, it seems better from the practical point of view to prefer the name "prayer of transforming union." It is better from the practical point of view because of the difficulties with the term "spiritual marriage" which have been mentioned earlier. It is difficult to use this name without implying the connotation of a special mystical experience, or expecting it, since it has sometimes been granted.

"The prayer of transforming union" also has a difficulty, although one less apt to disturb. This prayer, like all contemplative prayer, may be hard to identify specifically in each case, and also may be given transiently to one who does not have the heroic degree of the virtues. As a result, some people may think that an experience of this prayer (or something which they think to be this prayer) denotes real sanctity, whereas many trials and much purification will ordinarily be necessary.

This difficulty can be met with the fact that the degree of sanctifying grace and the degree of prayer are not necessarily connected. Even the total absence of such prayer does not of itself argue against the higher (and deeper) spiritual state in sanctifying grace. All that the habitual state of this prayer can indicate is a strong probability that there is a correlation deep in the soul. To have moral certainty, there would also have to be the heroic degree of the virtues.

In favor of the name, "prayer of the transforming union" it can be said that this name is clearly descriptive of the essential elements perceived in this prayer. Basically there is union. Thus, this word describes the general classification of the prayer. That is, it belongs to the prayer of union and thereby does away with much of the uncertainty over what in general the prayer is. But even more, the conscious union itself is now seen as so great in comparison with what has been experienced before, that the soul feels completed and fulfilled by an instinctive consciousness of a personal ultimate. The conscious oneness with its All can seemingly become no greater on this earth.

The union is also recognized as permanent, despite the frailty which the soul deeply knows it has (See *Interior Castle*, VII, 1, 2). Indeed because it is aware of this permanent kind of union, it is all the more careful in regard to venial sin, deliberate imperfections, and voluntarily remiss acts. In this permanence, "union" is fully in harmony with the metaphor of marriage; the soul knows the security of its state in the love of the Beloved.

Despite this possible opening toward presumption, this prayer is indeed an advance. While the soul was in the admittedly great prayerful union of ecstasy and rapture, it could not be wholly confident, even from the natural point of view, when the familiar contact with the outer world was taken from it, even snatched away abruptly. The new union brings a deep security which St. Teresa tells us "can be frightened at nothing" (*Ib.*, VII, 30).

Yet this is too superficial a reason to explain the new confident oneness. Surely the primary reason is the greater love shown by God. But nevertheless there should be certain reenforcing graces working on human nature so that mystical union not be a miracle. This abatement of the ecstasies and raptures may also come about because of the ability to overcome or transcend the fears arising from the spiritual and psychological causes mentioned earlier. Closer union is therefore a work of further purification, usually a work both of grace and nature. Any psychological liberation of course must remain subordinate to the spiritual union. It can never become a more primary end nor an end in itself.

We may thus come to experience that our reasons for fear are not as formidable as they seemed. Perhaps even more effectively, our will receives the grace to live this knowledge. Any purification will be accompanied by a certain increase of humility, inducing us to accept the weaknesses of our human condition instead of perhaps recoiling from them blindly because of a deep and as yet unresolved pride. Indeed some of the outpouring of the psyche in the Dark Night may still occur to accomplish our purification from deep, internal obstacles to God. There is a possible indication of this in the last stage of the mystical life in a strange and repeated experience of St. Teresa of Avila, who does not seem to have gone through the Dark Night of the Spirit as classically described by St. John of the Cross (See *Interior Castle*, VII, 4).

The concept of oneness (abstractly considered) has many degrees from absolute unity to the faintest similarity. The appropriateness of the term "prayer of transforming union" is especially shown in that here the union is brought about by a transformation, in this case a transformation called deification, that is, by the soul's perceiving that its oneness with God is a becoming like God.

We have already seen several instances of this inner perception of deification and it will help to repeat two of them here in order to make clear what this impression is. "It is like water descending from heaven into a river or spring, where one is so mixed with the other that it *cannot be discovered which* is the river and which is the rain water" (*Interior Castle*, VII, 2). Or an opposite kind of metaphor: "This divine light acts upon the soul . . . in the same way as fire acts upon a log of wood in order *to transform it into itself*" (*Dark Night*, II, 19).

Earlier we wrote at length on such expressions which seem to imply identity with God. What we said there in the context of the basic union and deification of sanctifying grace also applies here. Now we are concerned principally with the *mystical perception* of this same relationship with God as given in prayer.

The process of basic spiritual transformation, the transformation of our mind and will into Christ, has been going on and accelerating for perhaps some long time since the beginning of our close following of Christ and our first desires for greater personal union with God. This was a work of grace on the part of God and of conscious effort at imitation on ours. This transformation into Christ is generally in the same order of the spiritual life as the virtues. The mystical transformation, while not diverse from the essentials of Christian conduct and sanctifying grace, is rather an intuitive and growing experience of the same union in deeply conscious love from God.

In the ordinary development of contemplative prayer to these highest levels the soul leaves behind at the moment of prayer the theological concepts of grace, which nevertheless express enormous truths which God has revealed to us. It intimately and personally experiences what others have only by faith. The result here is a deep sense of divinization which principally constitutes the transforming union *mystically*, even if this is not the constant emphasis of every mystical experience in this union.

This divinization, along with a sense of permanence, can be said to be the specific difference between the transforming union and previous mystical states, always allowing for degrees of it, and allowing also for possible impressions of it earlier and transiently. These latter are not surprising since the soul is in sanctifying (that is, divinizing) grace in all its previous contemplative prayer. To be considered authentic this ultimate mystical union must be confirmed by external criteria, especially by the heroic degree of the virtues.

The recognition of this state is intuitive. God is able to make us understand it by his supreme power over us, just as in contemplative prayer itself he is able to make us understand wordlessly that it is he. All that can be said about recognizing it is that the soul understands that it has reached some kind of maximum, always allowing for degrees of greater or less in this maximum range. It sees this in the inarticulate manner of all contemplative prayer, that is, not by clear ideas (such as the mystic may try to express later) but rather in an overwhelming experience of closest union and likeness and love.

We who do not have this intuition (and also the mystics themselves at the times they do not have it) are compelled to pursue our way by the sure principles of faith and right reason. Indeed, so sure are these principles that we must judge all alleged experiences and the expressions of all mystical experiences by means of what God has given us through revelation and through the Church in its extraordinary and ordinary teaching mission. Thus, for instance, did the Church judge in its just condemnation of Eckhart.

This experience of deification does not contradict the Sacred Scripture nor the teachings of the Church nor the sound theological reasoning. Contradictions can result from a looseness of expression of one less gifted in words than in interior experiences, from a lack of careful preciseness, or from an attempt (perhaps unconscious) to fit the experience into contaminated theological ideas as if the water from a pure spring were to flow over the rotting carcass of a dead animal. Any of these may bring forth faulty descriptions. The truth is that authentic mystical experience of deification flows easily and clearly from the doctrine of sanctifying grace, as the Scripture plainly tells us, that we "become sharers of the divine nature" (2 P 1:4).

This sharing in the nature of God is by way of likeness, something again demanded by the Scripture in telling us of our adoption as sons (e.g., Jn 1:12; Rm 8:15). Adoption and sonship demand some likeness in nature to the one adopting. For instance, people have been known to become very much attached to their pets but they still cannot adopt these as they could a homeless child.

Just as there is a minimum degree of this likeness with God (presumably that of a newly baptized infant) so are there maximum degrees. These latter are fixed by the will of God. Likeness to God is capable of endless increase (though it can never, by addition of even endless degrees of created perfection, become the equal of him whose uncreated nature is beyond all measuring by degrees). In this sense, in always a limited and created sense, we can speak of all those in sanctifying grace as being deified, but especially those in the transforming union. What the prayer of transforming union does is to allow the soul to experience the indefinable godlikeness that faith and the heroic degree of the virtues tell us is truly there.

This superlative godlikeness can be more easily understood by the example of the reflection of the sun in a mirror made of polished gold metal. While gold in any state will reflect the sun, in order to have the best reflection, the surface of the mirror can have no impurity on it and must be perfectly smooth and highly polished. When nothing but the reflection of the uncreated God can be found in the soul, and no impurity or imperfection seen in it, but only the God that it reflects, the soul will indeed be beautiful with the beauty coming from the uncreated and surpassingly infinite beauty of God.

This reflection shines brightly by the soul's being polished by constant love, by doing the will of God in love, and by using the many means of grace. Sanctifying grace increases in the soul, not as a box is filled with various jewels, but by the reflection's being made brighter: the soul becomes more and more like God, without deformity or blemish, without reservation in giving itself to God, and with great love.

To speak in theological words what the soul in mystical union intuitively understands without words, and understands all at one glance, we repeat that the likeness is not identity of being or nature (just as the mirror is not the sun), but according to what is called analogy of being: the soul sees itself sharing in God in its own way what God *is* in his own way. In every analogy there is something similar and something different. For instance, we may call a certain man a lion because he has a powerful personality, even though there are obvious differences between him and a real lion. In any comparison between God and ourselves the differences of course are incalculable and almost completely indescribable.

The remarkable and almost unbelievable thing about our elevation in grace is that by sharing in God's nature, the differences are somewhat obliterated, not in reality because we will always be creatures and totally dependent beings, but rather in appearance—if we can use such a crude word to describe it. The comparison with the homeless child will help us.

After adoption the child is treated with great love by his parents and is given food, clothing, and shelter such as he never dreamed of having. The parents, like God, are wealthy and powerful. His new dignity will also become apparent in his attitudes, bearing, and way of acting, and this will be noticeable to a discerning observer.

If the child were an ideal person, as is the case in the transforming union, there would be little observable difference between him and a child of the same blood as the parents, so completely would he become a part of the family. Yet underneath these appearances, there would always be his origin and total dependence, realities which make him a different blood and condition from his parents. However, the parents are so good and the mutual love is so great that the child never thinks of this when he is with them, even when he has so much evidence of their dignity and splendor. For him, at this closeness, he has become one with them in all they are and possess.

Sanctifying grace, especially in the high degree that the mystic sees in the transforming union, makes us something so indescribably good that, when we have to speak about it, we are forced to liken it to what is totally indescribable in itself, the goodness that is God. Weak and poor, we become like God, just as the mirror becomes something dazzlingly more when the sun shines upon it.

Since this experience of likeness to God is usually given only to those who are very close to God in grace as well as in prayer, one might ask why it was not given earlier. The reason may be that the soul in its uncleanness would normally shrink from God, as perhaps it somewhat does in the dark contemplation which purifies it especially in the earlier stages of the life of prayer. This aversion is to some extent like our human experience of self-revelation. Most of us have difficulty in seeing our deeper imperfections because we are unconsciously afraid to look.

Since the recognition of the transforming union in prayer is by intuition, we must accept the resulting fact that there are few mystical criteria. This ought to be expected by the very nature of contemplative prayer which cannot be externally proven. For instance, if I see a rainbow, I can prove it by taking someone outside and pointing it out. But the mystic obviously cannot take anyone inside his mind. Thus, when he tells us that the soul "appears to be God," or (in metaphor) that, "enlightened to the greatest possible extent, (it) appears to be light itself" (*Living Flame*, I, 13) we must accept this internally observable deification as the essential criterion which we ourselves will be given if God draws us by this way.

And yet in this prayer of transforming union we do not seek deification as such nor do we usually avert to it. As in all contemplative prayer, even the lowest, we seek God for himself; in comparison with him we seek nothing else. God is ever our object; he is the wonder and love that is our delight. The simple thing that all contemplative prayer is, from highest to lowest, more vividly true here. The likeness to God, the union with him, and the deification all bring God. Our joy is in him and not primarily in any personal perfection. We still pour ourselves into him. We still rest only in his love.

One other indication, apparently more accessible, for the recognition of the mystical state of transforming union is given by St. John of the Cross. This insight comes by observing the manner of the soul's operations, the transformation of the faculties of the soul by the divine mode of action. "All the movements and operations and inclinations which the soul had aforetime, and which belonged to the principle and strength of its natural life are now in this union changed into Divine movements . . . moved wholly by the Spirit of God, even as St. Paul teaches, saying 'That they that are moved by the Spirit of God are the sons of God himself.' So the understanding of this soul is now the understanding of God; its will is the will of God; and its memory is the memory of God; and its delight is the delight of God" (*Living Flame*, II, 34).

We can safely say that the saint had a conscious awareness, through contemplative prayer, of this transformation or deification of his spiritual faculties and their operations. On the other hand, he is at the same time accurately describing the state of the perfect soul which does not have this assurance through contemplative prayer but rather through comparing its internal and external actions to the theological teaching on the gifts of the Holy Spirit. Indeed St. John of the Cross tells this to us clearly, even though in his usual absolute manner of "the most" and "the highest": "Therefore the soul can perform no acts, but it is the Holy Spirit that performs them and moves it to perform them" (*Ib.*, I, 4). We see that the intuitive observation of the mystic and the theological reasoning on the gifts of the Holy Spirit are identical. We have a sure linkage with the external criteria of the transforming union as a spiritual state which is based on the gifts but manifests itself here in the effects of the heroic degree of the virtues.

As with anything in the spiritual life we must discern the true from the false by its effects. This is especially necessary with contemplative prayer since this takes place so deep in the soul that it cannot be observed directly, not even by the soul itself. As soon as it begins to examine the prayer, its act of judging destroys the simple intuition which is required for the prayer (See St. Francis de Sales, *op. cit.*, VI, 10). Objective criteria for the higher degrees of contemplative prayer are the more necessary because the phenomena and the resulting account of what was experienced are not above counterfeit, unconscious if in no other way, and not excluding the action of the devil.

When we come to specific effects for the highest kinds of contemplative prayer, we are sometimes met with lists of graces which are alleged for each degree. This will be particularly noticeable if we read St. Teresa's later mansions or summaries made from them. There we sometimes find the same grace listed in more than one place, for instance, graces in regard to suffering and abandonment to God's will. This is not surprising, and we must not blame St. Teresa. We must expect that any kind of close contact with God will produce similar effects, although progressively deeper. Of course, her descriptions are in great part autobiographical.

A danger of this cataloging and accepting the personal for the universal is that some person or some director will read these effects or experiences as described, and will approve or disapprove a state of prayer because of the literal reading of the words. But some of these can be easily counterfeited, even unconsciously. For instance, the indifference to life or death for the love of God can drop from the tongue quite readily.

On the contrary, some of these alleged effects of, or experiences in, higher mystical prayer may be missing. For example, a man may be so weighed down by ill health or many occupations that every day is a heroic survival, and yet he may feel no ardent zeal to be off doing something for his neighbor. Rather his heroism may be found in his willingness to be offered completely in his present situation for the Church and for the world. These good effects as described have no real connection with any state of prayer and therefore do not necessarily denote it; there is not one of them that cannot be produced by grace alone without any contemplative prayer whatsoever.

The objective effects to be looked for are the solid virtues in the ever-increasing measure of the heroic degree, though not without fluctuations even here. The composite of these cannot be counterfeited. Contemplative prayer is an excellent means to acquire them, and an excellent means to increase in grace and to dispose ourselves to receive the great graces from the Mass and the sacraments more fruitfully.

Therefore, instead of an arbitrary set of specific moral and spiritual characteristics drawn from the experiences of another, it seems more consonant with the doctrine of personal vocation, the calling to be one's true self, to expect not only that each person will develop in all the virtues and along the lines of the fruits of the Holy Spirit and the beatitudes, but also that even here on the highest level of the spiritual life God will emphasize certain qualities according as he has called and developed each individual from the beginning. Indeed he has done this in each of the great mystics.

It is perhaps a disappointment to be given only very general criteria for the prayer of the transforming union and to have to leave so much to the personal intuition of the soul when in this state. On the other hand, however, if we read the descriptions of the mystics, we will still not be very much more enlightened. Those who attempt to describe are still forced to use words which they admit do not describe (See *Living Flame*, IV, 17), or they turn to metaphor or to poetry. These descriptions will not be remembered anyway, and for the soul who really loves, one moment with God in any degree of conscious union is worth more than all the descriptions.

The descriptions are only a small help for the soul to advance, and indeed may hold it back. To be in the highest spiritual state means relatively complete absence of self-consciousness in our relationship with God. It means above all, desiring him for his own sake, and successfully becoming more like him in sanctifying grace and the virtues. In respect to sanctifying grace we have the degree of closeness to God which we will be taking with us to heaven for eternity. Whether on earth we have been giving the highest possible prayer or not will be much less important than this.

Even though this is the highest state of prayer, we must not make the mistake of thinking that it is always at its highest degree of intensity. St. Teresa of Avila, who had already experienced all the states of prayer and much that was extraordinary besides, was speaking of her present condition when in her *Life* (ch. 17) she describes what is essentially the prayer of quiet, the lowest form of clearer contemplation.

It may be that when the saints proclaimed that they were imperfect, they were speaking not only of their internal and external imperfection, but also of their life of prayer. We like to think of the saints as giants who gazed heavenward with a steady, entranced absorption. Yet when we know, as from the life of St. Thérèse of Lisieux, that a saint can be in total darkness, we can presume that prayer in the later unitive way is not necessarily a constantly luminous experience either. Indeed at any stage of the life of prayer we must not expect that the general daily experience will be the highest kind of prayer that has been given us.

The Divine Lover is also Divine Wisdom, and although he may draw us very close and into the deeper understanding of his mysteries, he remembers our human condition of frailty. Indeed it is a paradox that, despite the deification of the soul and its operations and despite the implicit acceptance of an indissoluble union, that is, that his love will hold us in perseverance until the end, the soul "does not consider itself safe" nor is it necessarily free from "great distress" (*Interior Castle*, VII, 2). These graces induce humility as well as greater love, and the validity of the union is proven by the humility as well as (and inseparably from) the love. Paradoxically again, the greater the sense of godlikeness, the greater awareness of poverty and total dependence.

In the transforming union as a spiritual state the experience of divinization may be limited in an individual to the essential awareness of the operation of the gifts of the Holy Spirit. The internal assurance of final perseverance in perfection may be understood as the bare operation of the virtue of hope. But here in the union as a mystical experience we may presume, if God calls us in this manner, that in a relationship which justly uses marriage as its most appropriate metaphor, many spiritual intimacies will be given by the Bridegroom. He does not have to do this, and his individual plan for a given soul may include very little of such delight, even with souls who are among the closest to him in grace.

In the context of the mystical life there is a certain presumption that God will not marry a soul, so to speak, and then not show it exclusive, most intimate, and even extraordinary manifestations of his love in deep penetration into himself and his mysteries. Whatever this will be in an individual case, we must accept the presumption that this is normal for this soul, even as would be the intimacies of greatly endowed lovers in marriage.

Similar to the beatific vision though mystical prayer may sometimes appear, especially in its higher degrees, it is principally a means to the deeper interior perfection of soul begun in our baptism. For this perfection God has other means, less delightful it is true, which he can use in his love, wisdom, and freedom. And yet, mystical experience is not only a means. It is the high point of human life as we measure it by experiencing love. If seeing him here, at best "through a glass darkly," can be this delight, what then must it be "face to face"?